Anonymous

Irish Faith in America

Recollections of a Missionary

Anonymous

Irish Faith in America
Recollections of a Missionary

ISBN/EAN: 9783337126148

Printed in Europe, USA, Canada, Australia, Japan

Cover: Foto ©Lupo / pixelio.de

More available books at **www.hansebooks.com**

"Ireland's tree of Catholicity never yielded to any blast; never did she lose a branch, nor a leaf. Never did she bend before the storm, and she raises her head to-day as graceful, as beautiful, as loaded with every flower of promise and fruit of fulfilment as in the day when the dying hand of Patrick waved its last benediction over her, and when with his fainting and dying voice he made his last prayer to God that Ireland might keep her faith until the end of time."—*Father Burke.*

IRISH FAITH

IN

AMERICA

RECOLLECTIONS OF A MISSIONARY.

TRANSLATED FROM THE FRENCH

By Miss ELLA McMAHON.

NEW YORK, CINCINNATI, AND ST. LOUIS:
BENZIGER BROTHERS,
Printers to the Holy Apostolic See.

To His Grace

The Most Rev. N. J. PERCHÉ,

Archbishop of New Orleans.

Your Grace:

To whom, more fitly than to you, can I dedicate this my first and humble work, in which I have endeavored to relate a few of the marvels of the faith of this missionary people in America, among whom you yourself have been an apostle for nearly half a century, and who to-day form a cherished portion of the flock confided to your care?

I am happy to lay at your feet this simple tribute of my homage; happier still if your Grace will deign to accept it as a mark of the sincere devotion of a fellow-laborer, and the deep affection of a son in Christ.

H. L.

My Very Reverend Fellow-laborer and dear Son in Christ:

I willingly accept the dedication of a study, the subject and object of which are equally dear to us both.

People, like individuals, have each a vocation to follow and a mission to fulfil. The mission of the Irish people, a noble and holy mission among all others, is that of propagating and maintaining the Catholic faith.

You show by incontestable facts this vocation of the Irish people, and the manner in which they fulfil their mission in the United States, a country which particularly interests us; but history tells that in every missionary country, as in the United States, the Irish, with invincible energy and untiring perseverance, have proved themselves the firm supporters and propagators of the Catholic faith.

You justly recall how dear to me is that portion of my flock which belongs to the Irish nation.

I most earnestly invoke God's blessing, my

dear son, upon you and your work, which will contribute to develop in hearts devotion to the Catholic faith.

✝ N. J. Perché,
Archbishop of New Orleans.

CONTENTS.

	PAGE
DEDICATION	5
LETTER OF MOST REV. ARCHBISHOP PERCHÉ	7

CHAPTER I.
America—Her Progress—True Liberty................... 11

CHAPTER II.
Mission of the Irish People—Lacordaire—Cardinal Newman—Dupanloup................................ 22

CHAPTER III.
Human Respect—Demonstrative Faith of the Irish—St. Patrick's Day Parade—O'Connell—Antiquity of Exterior Forms of Worship....................... 25

CHAPTER IV.
The Irish a Missionary People par Excellence—Their Zeal in Propagating the Faith.............. 43

CHAPTER V.
Zeal of the Irish in defending their Faith—Archbishop Hughes. 56

CHAPTER VI.
The Simple, Trustful Faith of the Irish—Their Veneration and Respect for Holy Things—Their Unlimited Confidence in their Priests and the Sacramentals of the Church.................................. 61

CHAPTER VII.
Strength of the Irish Faith at the Hour of Death—Zeal of the Irish for the Reputation of the Clergy................. 83

CHAPTER VIII.
Generosity of the Irish Faith—The New Cathedral of New York—Extracts from the "Letters of a Young Irishwoman to her Sister"............................. 92

CHAPTER IX.
Death of Henri de Kleist, a Disciple of Kant—Death of Theophane Venard, Apostolic Missionary.............. 116

CONTENTS.

CHAPTER X.

How deservedly Ireland Merits the Title of the "Virgin Isle" —Her Characteristic Virtue............................ 121

CHAPTER XI.

Patriotism of the Irish—Imperishable Love for the Mother-Country........ 127

CHAPTER XII.

The Confraternity of the Immaculate Heart of Mary in New York—Its Establishment in Chicago...................... 135

CHAPTER XIII.

Whence the Irish Reap the Numerous and Eminent Qualities of their Faith—Their Vigilant Observance of Religious Practices—The Heroic Constancy which Ireland has Displayed in the Defence of her Faith Unrivalled in the Annals of Mankind—Association for the Catholic Colonization of the Irish in America............................ 142

CHAPTER XIV.

How the Faith of the Irish Enables them to Triumph over their National Failing.................................. 156

CHAPTER XV.

The Sympathy and Union which have always Existed between the Irish and the French—Extract from "The Letters of a Young Irishwoman to her Sister"—The Wit of the Irish in Repartee—Letter of the Nun of Kenmare.............. 162

CHAPTER XVI.

Souls the True Riches of a People—True Progress through the Teachings of Christ—Heroism of the Christian Brothers during the Franco-Prussian War........................ 200

CHAPTER XVII.

Lever of Archimedes—Macaulay—Lacordaire—Ireland—Poland.. 212

CHAPTER XVIII.

The Ancient Problem—Its Solution, the Decalogue—Jouffroy —Incredulity Tends to Depopulate Heaven and Disenchant Earth... 215

CHAPTER XIX.

The Enemies of Faith—What Faith has Done for Them..... 220

IRISH FAITH IN AMERICA.

CHAPTER I.

AMERICA—HER PROGRESS—TRUE LIBERTY.

MUCH has been written of America. It is a country of which a great deal of good and a great deal of evil has been written. Some have extravagantly praised it, others have vehemently reviled.

Is America that terrestrial paradise depicted to us by passionate adorers of that new country, who saw there only incomparable virtues unmixed with vice?

Is America, on the contrary, that hell in anticipation where other prejudiced and extravagant minds pretend to find only injustice and crimes of every description?

To be just, to be true, in being truly and coldly impartial, we must recognize that America is neither one nor the other; it contains neither so much grandeur nor so much baseness ; the country merits

"Ni cet excès d'honneur, ni cette indignité." *

It is not the Eden of old, for the simple reason that Paradise was forever lost to us by our first parents. Never can there be found again a cloudless horizon, or complete perfection, either in the new world or the old.

Nor is it the hell which some depict, for if vice is found there, honor is also paid to virtue ; good and evil exist side by side ; there is a mixture of both, as there ever is wherever men are free.

It will certainly be interesting to see how this can be elucidated.

But at the present time, when things material so prominently hold the attention of the world, the authors generally who have written on America have not cared to invite their readers to an examination so severe, or to assist them in the solution of problems so grave.

Some have chiefly endeavored to prove that the New World is a country where everything is grand—nature, ideas, enterprises, men, and things.

They have told us : It is the country which

---

* Neither this excess of honor, nor this indignity.

enjoys the distinction of containing the greatest river in the world, the Mississippi, with its 3000 miles of navigable waters.

It is the country which possesses the grandest cataract in the world, the Falls of Niagara, where the waters of four great lakes unite and fall from a height of more than 160 feet.

It is the country where the traveller finds the most colossal railway, the line from San Francisco to New York, 3400 miles in length, or about the distance from one continent to another, from Havre to New York.

It is the country where the most remarkable bridge in the world commands the admiration of the stranger—the Victoria bridge on the St. Lawrence in Montreal, nearly two miles in length. Moreover, New York will soon be united to Brooklyn by a bridge still more remarkable. It will measure 5989 feet in length, and 200 feet in height, and will cost over thirteen millions. This gives an elevation as high as the towers of Notre Dame, surmounted by a six-story building.

Others, absorbed in the feverish agitations of an age which pursues and dreams only of material progress, have chiefly endeavored to show that America has given to the world more than three fourths of our modern inventions.

It was in fact an American who, ruling the

storms and tempests, so to speak, chaining the waves and tides, first made them subservient to human industry by the invention of the steamboat.

It is owing to an American that we are able to guide the thunderbolt, and to flash our thoughts with the rapidity of lightning from one end of the globe to the other; for it was an American who gave us the lightning rod and the electric telegraph.

To the inventive genius of an American, again, the sick should be forever grateful; so too the workwoman and the tiller of the field, for it was an American who discovered chloroform and invented the sewing machine, the reaper and the mower.

America, finally. it is generally said, is the country which has the most institutions of every kind; the most numerous industries, and the greatest business; most work and most happiness; the greatest number of inventions, machines, amusements, newspapers; the most money and the most comfort — a few may whisper, and the most injustice, the greatest number of thieves and criminals—but all must agree in proclaiming that she has made the greatest progress and enjoys the truest liberty. Generally, writers stop here; they go no higher. Either they have not seen, or they were unwilling to recognize that, side by side with this purely material progress, which is incontestable and cannot be denied in America, there is, particularly at the present time, a daily increasing progress fully as remarkable in another sense, and truly worthy of admiration. In our day it has already produced and will continue to produce the most serious effects on this people.

At the beginning of the century the illustrious Count de Maistre said America was a child in "swaddling clothes." He was speaking particularly of the great material prosperity of a people who at that time hardly numbered four millions. The Christian Plato could have applied the same term no less truly to another more important progress upon which the moral greatness as well as the happiness of a people depend, the progress through Jesus Christ and His gospel ; for from this period, that is, from the day her chains were broken, the Catholic faith has advanced with giant strides. If America, as everything seems to indicate, continues this march of progress, a day will come when we can say of her, what the same Count de Maistre said of Europe: "She has only reached this high civilization because she began by theology."

The present state of the Old World gives a

special interest to the study of this real progress through the gospel, the only one worthy of the name of progress, that which is now witnessed in America.

In the Old World a false democracy, a Voltairean press, an impious and spurious science, have united to raise a rampart against their common enemy, the only obstacle to the realization of their guilty and insensate dreams; and with the folly of one who would turn the sun from its course, they cease not to cry out, each after his own fashion: *Catholic Church, thy reign is ended; thou shalt go no further!*

And in the New World another truer, more earnest, and, above all, a more liberal democracy grants the same Church absolute freedom, not through indifference or contempt, but through respect for religion and the sacred rights of conscience. In the language of one of the governors of New York, she exclaims: *We must ever remember that justice elevates nations.*

At Paris the Municipal Council, utterly disregarding the urgent claims of families, with one stroke of the pen tyrannically closes the schools of religious societies. In Chicago, on the contrary, the Municipal Council unanimously accede to the closing of one of the streets of their great city in order that the same society may enlarge their college, already a vast one, yet too small to meet the demands of the population.

In France, the President of the Republic signs a decree granting a delay of three months to the association or congregation, so called, of Jesus, to disperse and vacate the establishments it occupies in the territory of the Republic. And in America the President of the Republic cordially accepts the seat of honor at the commencement in the college of the same Jesuits, near Washington, the seat of government. He there makes a speech in which he renders public homage to the zeal and devotion as well as the patriotism of these experienced professors ; he praises their method of teaching, and points out their success amid the applause of the best society, both Protestants and Catholics, who assemble in large numbers at a spectacle of this kind, which appears to them very natural because it appears simply just.

Here they are endeavoring to re-enkindle with new ardor and ever-increasing injustice the old war against liberty of teaching. In America, on the contrary, if Catholics desire to erect a university beside their new cathedral in New York, or Boston, or Philadelphia, or any other great city of the Union, Jews, Protestants, Quakers, Freemasons, Infidels, Mormons, liberally come forward to the assistance of their Catholic brethren, thus eloquently manifesting to the astonished European that it is honoring one's self and one's country to favor the diffusion of science and light, whoever may be the distributors of these gifts.

Here, in a land eighteen centuries old in Catholicism, the Sovereign Pontiff is obliged to proceed with the utmost prudence for fear of wounding the susceptibilities of the ruling powers, whenever there is question of taking any measure conscientiously judged necessary for the good of the Church and the salvation of souls. In America, for the last century—that is, since the nation became an independent people—the Sovereign Pontiff has not yet encountered the slightest opposition from the government. He convokes councils, multiplies episcopal sees, creates cardinals without any obstacle, amid the applause of all. And to-day Leo. XIII., so gloriously reigning, can say with as much and even more truth than Gregory XVI. : "Nowhere do I find myself more a Pope than in the United States of America."

In a word, finally, people and rulers in the old continent have madly rejected the ancient traditions which have made their country great and illustrious. Ready to overthrow the most sacred monuments of centuries in the false name of modern progress, they furiously attack the only divine institution of which they have the greatest need in order to live and prosper.

And America aids the rapid progress of this same institution in her midst, not only peacefully and without fear, but with pride and ambition. She fearlessly beholds its triumphal march ; she applauds the daily and ever-increasing victories of the Catholic apostolate, seeing it advance with giant strides to the near and glorious future which is reserved for it. Behold the remarkable but veritable progress which, particularly in our day, is to be noted in America ; and it is precisely because the Old World systematically rejects it that it is more flourishing and more marvellous in the new.

Faith is by nature a great traveller. Issuing from the crib of the Saviour in the East and rejected by the Jews, she traverses the waters and swiftly implants herself in Rome, the capital of the known world. Then, scaling the Alps more valiantly than Julius Cæsar and his numerous legions, she also in her turn conquers Gaul. "It is she who has made France. She has held France in her arms, so to speak, as a mother holds her child, guiding her steps through the barbarous ages, gradually softening her morals in proportion as she instils the light of truth into the souls of her children, while forming the mind and cultivating the intelligence."*

But if, in our turn, we, the sons of Faith, ungratefully and unjustly repudiate our mother; if, blushing for her and refusing to recognize her, we drive her as a stepmother from our hearths, she, who has no need of us, will continue her grand progress. Spiritual planet, destined to bear the torch of truth to all nations, "thou art the light of the world!" Like the terrestrial sun to which she is likened, her course will ever speed from the east to the west; she will traverse the waves to fix her tent in the midst of a new people and take up her abode in new lands. This is the history of centuries. When a nation no longer accepts the faith, Jesus Christ, the author of faith, takes His cross, His priesthood, and His sacraments, and goes to the depths of forests and unknown countries where other nations call Him and impatiently hold forth their arms to receive Him with gratitude, joy, and happiness.

This is exactly what is happening at present in America.

Therefore, Fenelon, the illustrious Bishop of Cambrai, tells us, "when you see vast regions

---

* M. De Mun au Cirque d'hiver 10 Juillet, 1879.

which suddenly open up a new world unknown to the old and greater than itself, believe not that so vast a discovery is due solely to the adventurous spirit of man. God accedes to human passions, however prominent they may appear in a work, only what is necessary to make them the instruments of His designs; thus man acts and God leads; and while the clouds are darkening about us the Catholic faith planted in America, in spite of many storms, ceases not to bring forth fruit."

Behold the marvellous fact which the good bishop records as early as his time, and of which I would say something for the edification of souls.

In the pages of my first and modest work, I shall try by the eloquence of facts to render homage to a nation of generous laborers and intrepid pioneers of the faith. Each day they plant it with zeal in this new vineyard of the Lord, and everywhere cause it to take deep root in this new and fruitful soil. Humble before men, they are great before God; for whose glory they earnestly and ardently labor. Almost unconsciously they labor also for the true greatness of their adopted country; it is thus the servers of God are the servers of men.

CHAPTER II.

MISSION OF THE IRISH PEOPLE—LACORDAIRE —CARDINAL NEWMAN—DUPANLOUP.

IF, as everything leads us to believe, the day is not far distant when the entire people of this New World, so varied in origin, language, and worship, religiously so agitated, comes to rest under this majestic tree called the Catholic Church, they must thank all those who sowed the grain of mustard seed; they will owe a special and most fervent thanksgiving to a whole nation who may well be called the MISSIONARY PEOPLE *par excellence*. Its providential and unceasing emigration has produced in America, as it will everywhere, religiously speaking, the happiest and most consoling results.

Who is this missionary people prepared by God during centuries for this noble vocation of apostleship?

It is the people whom Lacordaire thus eloquently describes in the presence of an imposing audience: "I will not name the country, gentlemen, this dear and sacred country, this country stronger than death ; my lips are not sufficiently pure to utter her name ; but heaven knows her, the earth blesses her, all generous hearts have offered to her children love, a country, an asylum. . . . O heaven which looks down upon her, O land which knows her, O all ye spirits worthier and better than I, pronounce for me the sacred name of *Ireland !*"

Ireland ! that country of which an illustrious convert now wearing the Roman purple, Cardinal Newman, thus speaks : " Green Erin, a land both old and young—old in its Christianity, and young in its hopes of the future. It is a nation which received the faith before the Saxon set foot on the soil of England, and which has never allowed its light to be extinguished in its heart."

Ireland ! the country to which the celebrated Bishop Dupanloup in 1861, pleading the noble cause of its people before the large audience of St. Roch, paid this beautiful tribute : " European nations and mankind itself are justly proud of the Irish race ; I know not a people in whom patriotism, purity of morals, courageous faith, invincible fidelity, valor, conquering and civilizing ardor, unselfishness, patience, poetry, eloquence, combined with a hope which is ever buoyant, never cast down, a hope crowned by misfortune, shine out to the world with more striking yet sorrowful splendor."

Yes, the Irish people whose qualities are thus eloquently set forth by an authoritative voice, are foremost by the ardor of their faith in planting Catholicism in America. The Irish, in the words of an American paper, are the foundation stones of the American Church. Religion and civilization flourish under their feet.

CHAPTER III.

HUMAN RESPECT—DEMONSTRATIVE FAITH OF THE IRISH—ST. PATRICK'S DAY PARADE—O'CONNELL — ANTIQUITY OF EXTERIOR FORMS OF WORSHIP.

N the Old World generally, particularly France at the present day, there is an idol before which entire populations prostrate themselves. In mute fear they tremblingly offer it in servile homage all that is noblest and grandest in man here below, all that constitutes his royalty in creation, liberty, honesty, courage. This idol of the day, so degrading to man, is *human respect*.

In its primitive and true sense *human respect* is a virtue, for the word means *respect of man*. Created to the image of God, king of creation, in his own name as well as that of his Maker man can claim from his fellow-creatures a tribute of respect, the homage of a reserve due to his dignity. Why has not human respect always been defined the fear of doing evil in order not to offend the just? Why must it be defined: *ashamed of doing good* through fear of offending the wicked? It is the work of the evil one; human respect was made by him. The fear of the Lord is the beginning of wisdom, Holy Scripture tells us. In fact, God first enters a soul through fear, but faith and love soon follow, and the soul advances from virtue to virtue. The evil one in this also would imitate God. He says to himself, God draws souls to Himself by a fear which giveth life. I will have for my arms the fear of man which giveth death.

Colbert, a celebrated minister, on returning from a visit to the child Louis XIV., encountered in the palace an influential person who said to him: "Well! what do you think of our young prince?" "I think," said Colbert, "he has in him the making of four great kings, I think even the making of an honest man." Remarkable words! For in fact it is easier to make a king than a man. Give the first one who presents himself a well-organized army, a well-filled exchequer; surround him with able ministers; and you will have a great king. But the making of a man is another thing. What truly makes a man in the proper sense of the word? *Vir* in Latin, which is such a philosophic tongue, means *a man of heart*, and the expression which signifies courage, *virtus*, has the same derivation. That which constitutes a man is neither riches, nor honors, nor glory, nor power; nor is it mind, or even genius. To be a man is to be free in one's will and disposition; to be true in one's words; to be courageous in one's actions. Liberty, honesty, courage; behold what elevates the man! Slavery, hypocrisy, cowardice; behold what abases, lowers, and disfigures him! Behold what wrests the crown from his brow! behold what breaks the sceptre in his hand! behold what degrades him! And this is the work of him who bows before the all-powerful idol of the day, *human respect*. But the Irishman knows not how to bend before this hideous idol of opinion. Neither at home nor abroad does he ever sacrifice to the God of fear. He breaks not his triple crown by a triple degradation; always and everywhere he is free, true, and courageous; for he everywhere ostensibly carries his faith with him; he manifests it and imposes it as the soldier carries and imposes his flag. All are obliged to witness this faith, to endure it, to admire it, and frequently to embrace it; for the *Irish Faith* is above all a *demonstrative Faith*.

To appreciate this fact one should witness with his own eyes the astonishing spectacle which a great American city, New York for example, affords on the 17th of March, a day when the Church celebrates the feast of St. Patrick, first apostle and patron of Ireland.

If on this day, from ten in the morning until four in the afternoon, certain Europeans, and particularly Frenchmen, were magically transported to the streets of the populous imperial city of New York, what would they think and what would they say?

What would they say to see with their own eyes, in the midst of several hundred thousand spectators, eager to enjoy a spectacle ever ancient and always new—at least 80,000 Irishmen marching in double file, all ostensibly manifesting to the multitude their faith and their nationality — their faith by the shamrock * which each man wears in his button-hole, their nationality by the green sash on which is engraven a harp,† and which is worn across the

---

* The shamrock, a three-leaved clover, the emblem of the Irish Faith, seems to date back to the time of their first Apostle, St. Patrick. The saint, we are told, was one day preaching in the open air to the nobility of the country, then idolaters, and endeavoring to explain to them the mystery of the Holy Trinity by images and comparisons. Perceiving a three-leaved clover at his feet he detached a leaf from its stem and showing it to his audience he said: "There is an image of the Holy Trinity. God is one and threefold, in the sense that this clover leaf is at the same time one and three fold."

† The harp is the coat of arms of Catholic Ireland, in

shoulder. What would they say to see displayed in the suite of this great army of 80,000 men, banners of every color, shape, and description. And what banners! Every one represents the patrons of their respective parishes, or the holy protectors of their religious, moral, or civil associations. Here are some of the most prominent names : IMMACULATE CONCEPTION, TRANSFIGURATION, HOLY INNOCENTS, ST. GABRIEL, ST. JAMES, ST. MICHAEL, ST. PATRICK, ST. COLUMBANUS, ST. JEROME, ST. BRIDGET, ST. ROSE OF LIMA ; banners of the SOCIETIES OF ST. VINCENT OF PAUL, the temperance societies of FATHER MATHEW, etc., etc. And then, what would be the further astonishment of those who in the name of *liberty of worship* and freedom of the streets, forbid pilgrimages and processions of the Blessed Sacrament. What, I

memory of the Irish bards, who on the arrival of St Patrick formed an hereditary and sacerdotal caste. It was among these bards, by whom Celtic poetry was preserved, that St. Patrick after converting them, recruited his most faithful and fervent disciples. It is for this reason, says the learned historian of the Monks of the West, that the harp of the bards has remained the symbol and coat of arms of Catholic Ireland and that the old Irish melodies, revived by the plaintive, indignant muse of a patriot poet, still preserve a sympathetic prestige and are rarely evoked without drawing tears from the eyes of the priests, the peasants and the friends of Ireland.

repeat, would be their amazement could they personally witness the admirable order and perfect silence of that immense multitude of curious spectators, composed of men of every creed and men holding every variety of opinion—to say nothing of the interminable line of public and private carriages, omnibuses, and cars halted for at least an hour and a half with their crowd of passengers, who calmly see this *King-People* file before them, without uttering a word of complaint or menace, without manifesting the least sign of impatience.

Finally, what would our modern republicans say if, following the procession, they could see these 80,000 men respectfully uncover the head each time they pass a church on their march, or particularly if they could read in large letters on a triumphal arch erected in the wealthiest portion of the city this magnificent profession of faith: *He that shall deny me before men, I will also deny him before my Father who is in heaven.*

Where are we? I can hear the astonished Europeans exclaim. In truth all this represents but one thing—fanaticism.

No, it is not fanaticism! It is simply the image of a true republic, of which yours is but a vain semblance, a ridiculous imitation, an illegitimate offspring. It is a republic where every one is free to manifest his faith, his nationality, his convictions, his political and religious opinions, without the risk of seeing himself appear in the columns of an infamous paper, then in caricature held up to the ridicule and derision of the public, and sometimes, even, subjected to fine and imprisonment.

The Irish know this. With their yearly grand religious and political demonstration of the 17th of March they seem to proclaim to all : *We are Catholics and Irishmen, and do not blush for either of these glorious titles.*

This demonstration, moreover, excites general interest. Our compatriots do not fail to participate in the universal enthusiasm.

Here are the terms in which, on the 17th of March, 1871, a French paper, *Le Courrier des Etats-Unis*, announces to its readers the Irish parade of that day :

" ST. PATRICK. To-day is the feast of the glorious patron of Ireland, St. Patrick ; it is to be hoped the weather will be favorable, for every measure has been taken to celebrate the day with more splendor than in the preceding years. It is estimated that at least 80,000 Irishmen will walk in procession through the streets of New York in the following order :

' The procession will form on Second Avenue, extending on the right the length of

Fourteenth Street. At ten o'clock a cannon will be fired; at this signal the military portion of the procession, under the command of Col. James Cavanagh, will take the right of the civil bodies, which will form in columns by companies and march down Second Avenue to Second Street, and from Second Street to the Bowery, from the Bowery to Chatham Street, passing through the City Hall Park, where the Mayor and Common Council will review the parade; then the procession will march up Broadway to Union Square, across Fourteenth Street to Seventh Avenue, up Seventh Avenue to Twenty-third Street, across Twenty-third Street to First Avenue, and down First Avenue to Cooper Institute, where the parade will disband.

"Among emblems, allegorical figures, etc., there will be seen in to-morrow's procession a large picture representing the historical visit of the Irish chieftain O'Neil to Queen Elizabeth, in her palace at Westminster. Mention is also made of a marvellous colossal bust of O'Connell on a triumphal car drawn by ten white horses.

"The warm sympathy manifested by the Irish for France during the unfortunate crisis through which she has just passed, cannot fail to be acknowledged to day by the special interest which our compatriots will take in this year's celebration of the feast of St. Patrick. Many Frenchmen of New York will doubtless do themselves the honor of hoisting the Irish flag on their residences."

But it is not only upon grand occasions that the *Irish Faith* courageously manifests itself, but at all times, under the eye of God alone, it is ever the same *demonstrative faith.*

"You who visit this noble country," exclaims Monseigneur Dupanloup, "enter their churches and behold the people in prayer; these poor men and women bending almost to the earth and striking their breasts. Where will you find a livelier, a more striking image of adoration and annihilation of man before God? Can you hear unmoved, at the Elevation, their audible sighs and prayers for fathers, mothers, brothers, sons, their exiles, their sick?" *

And this lively and demonstrative faith is not confined solely to the peasants and children; no, the higher classes and chiefs of the people have always given the same noble example.

To cite but one of the most recent illustrations of this, let me recall to your mind O'Con-

---

* Sermon of Mgr. Dupanloup at St. Roch, 1861.

nell, that man who so justly won from his country the glorious name of Liberator, "that man of justice whose long and troubled career cost not one drop of blood, or even a tear, and who after moving more men and peoples than we find recorded in any history, descended to the tomb pure of all reproach, without fear that any living soul could raise his sepulchral stone and claim of him reparation—I do not say for one culpable action, but for a misfortune during the fifty years of his public life." *

A great admirer of this *man of justice* was frequently present at his oratorical triumphs in the House of Commons. During a severe winter, one Saturday evening in February, important debates were prolonged far into the night. O'Connell was the last to speak; as he had won the last triumph, and after speaking for two hours, until two o'clock in the morning, the house broke up. The admirer in question had frequently heard that O'Connell received Holy Communion on all Sundays and feast days in an humble Catholic chapel of London. On leaving Parliament at this early morning hour, he said to himself, "Here is a good opportunity of proving how far the celebrated Irish orator's fidelity to his religious habits will

---

* Sermon of Lacordaire at the funeral of O'Connell.

carry him." At six o'clock in bitter weather he softly opened the door of the little chapel and placed himself in a position to command a view of the whole congregation. He looked all about him, but perceived only some workmen and a few servants. It is very natural, he thought, that he should be absent; yesterday was such a fatiguing day, his speech was a very long one, and the session was prolonged so far into the night. But his eyes gradually becoming accustomed to the obscurity of the poor little chapel, he caught a glimpse of a commanding figure a little distance from him leaning against a column, and recognized O'Connell; at the moment of communion he took off his cloak, devoutly approached the holy table, and knelt in the midst of the poor women and servants.

This lively and demonstrative faith, shared alike by high and low, is what the Irish carry with them everywhere.

Let us transport ourselves for a moment to one of the fifty Catholic churches of New York at seven o'clock in the morning, during the celebration of the mass. We will not leave the church without recognizing the Irish, or without finding edification in their every act.

Behold them, when the sanctuary bell announces the moment of consecration; they raise their hands, they extend their arms in the form of a cross, they pray and sigh aloud ; at times some leave their pew and prostrate themselves in the aisle, in order to assume a more suppliant and adoring attitude. There, if you wait until the end of mass, you will be further edified. You will see them approach as near as possible to the high altar, before which they bow profoundly, making several genuflections, and frequently remain for a moment almost prostrate to the ground. From here they go to kneel at the altar of the Blessed Virgin, then before that of St. Joseph. Then follows a last and touching station before the body of the dead Christ which the Italians call the *pietà;* they pray here for a few moments, and respectfully press their lips to the five wounds of the Saviour. At the door of the church they take holy water, sign themselves with it repeatedly, and sprinkle their faces with it ; then turning toward the tabernacle they make a last genuflection, as if to bid farewell to our Lord, and finally withdraw. This is an invariable ceremony with the Irish on leaving the church. It preaches the faith so eloquently that though I witnessed it every day for many years, it was an ever-new spectacle to me, and never failed to move me deeply.

In fact I could not but think of the words of

one of their bishops : *They have taken everything from us but our faith.*

O grand people ! nation illustrious by the firmness of thy faith ! yes, truly, they have taken everything from thee : bread, home, family ; thy altars by robbing thee of thy cathedrals and perverting them to error, thy country by thrusting thee from thy mountains, thy lakes, thy green fields ; but they could not break the "sacred tie, nor interrupt that paternal embrace, nor efface the filial kiss which Ireland and the papacy exchanged by the hand of St. Celestin and the lips of St. Patrick." * Continue then, confessors of the Faith, to go through the world a living and perpetual souvenir of the middle ages, and say to the world : Yes, they have taken everything from us, yet they have taken nothing ; for in the midst of our exile and our privations God remains on our wooden altars, and the faith of our fathers in our hearts.

These exterior manifestations of a sincere faith may appear, even to some Christians, puerile, and tainted with superstition, exaggeration, and novelty.

To believe this one must be ignorant of the fact that there are no innovations in the tra-

* Mgr. Mermillod.

ditions of the Catholic Church; she simply preserves, ennobles, and explains them all. Therefore it was not the Church who established the custom of praying with the hands extended; Moses, David, and Solomon, those three illustrious figures of the New Testament, prayed with their hands raised to God. While the Jews struggled in the plain against the nations who opposed their entrance to the promised land, Moses prayed on the mountain with his hands raised to heaven; and when his hands were raised Israel advanced, but when he desisted Israel fell back. "*When Moses lifted up his hands, Israel overcame; but if he let them down a little, Amalec overcame*" (Ex. 17:11).

David, also, has given the example of this attitude of prayer. "*Let my prayer,*" he exclaims, "*be directed as incense in thy sight, the lifting up of my hands as evening sacrifice*" (Ps. 140:2). Solomon, on the day of the consecration of the most marvellous temple of ancient times, recalling the example of his father, falls on his knees in the presence of all Israel, and raising his hands to heaven thanks the Almighty for having deigned to choose a dwelling among them.

Does not St. Paul, himself in chains at Rome, address from his prison the same recommendation to Timothy: "*I will therefore that men pray in every place, lifting up pure hands without anger and contention"* (1 Tim. 2 : 8). The early Christians in the catacombs, the martyrs in the amphitheatres, faithful to the advice of the apostle, prayed with their hands raised to heaven, and Tertullian, sixteen hundred years ago, gives the reason for it : " By the elevation of hands we offer ourselves to God, freely placing ourselves at his disposition. The attitude of a Christian in prayer announces that he is ready to suffer everything in following the Divine Model of Calvary." Therefore we cannot say that this practice of the Irish is puerile or an innovation. Let us rather admire the fidelity of the nation in preserving in all their purity the pious and touching traditions of their fathers.

As to the genuflection before the tabernacle, it is wholly a natural consequence of faith. Among all nations the genuflection has always been regarded as an act of exterior adoration reserved for God alone. Pagan monarchs of the East and of Rome, in the delirium of their insensate pride, have not feared to claim this divine honor for themselves. But wherever there were found true adorers of the Most High they ever refused, after the example of the just Mordochai, to bend the knee to these gods of a day. At the peril of his life he remains standing while all the others prostrate themselves before the proud Aman. To him a genuflection, in the religious sense of the word, meant adoration. "Lord," he cries, "thou knowest all things, and thou knowest that it was not out of pride and contempt, or any desire of glory, that I refused to worship the proud Aman; for I would willingly and readily, for the salvation of Israel, have kissed even the steps of his feet; but I feared lest I should transfer the honor of my God to a man, and lest I should adore any one except my God." Since the genuflection, in a religious point of view, is an exterior act of worship, we need not be astonished to see it so frequently repeated among the Irish; we should rather be astonished at the conduct of those who have not the courage to imitate them. "If I could possess the faith of Catholics," said a Turk, a disciple of Mahomet, "and believe that God was in the tabernacle I would not only prostrate myself on entering the church, but I would go on my knees from the vestibule to the altar."

Therefore " the genuflection made before the Blessed Sacrament exposed on the altar or enclosed in the tabernacle, is in all Catholic countries a sacred custom, a universal rite which is faithfully observed. I should not say all Catholic countries, for there is one exception, and unfortunately it is France! In the greater number of the parishes and dioceses the faithful, even the best, those who come to church, are satisfied on entering and leaving to make an inclination of the head to our Lord, a sort of *familiar good-morning* or *patronizing salutation.*

" Even when done respectfully and conscientiously, which is not always the case, this inclination of the head does not suffice to attest our faith in the Real Presence. It is a sign of veneration which we owe to the relics on the altar, but it is not an act of adoration. The genuflection alone is an attestation of faith. Whence is it that the greater number neglect it, and that the eldest daughter of the Church is so remiss among all her sisters? We are not rash in attributing it to Gallicanism and Jansenism. These two principles of pride have roused us into a state of insubordination to the Church, causing us to despise her most venerated customs, disfigure public prayer, trample under foot our most ancient traditions, deprive our Church of a head by repudiating her direct apostolic authority, and finally, for more than a hundred years, to verge upon schism and even heresy.

" Now that, thanks to a return to Roman unity, the usurping reign of liturgical anarchy is abolished, it is a duty to abandon the last remnant of the shameful inheritance of Gallicanism and Jansenism. Let us cease to mingle a discordant voice with the united harmony of the Church. Let Catholic England, Spain, and Italy find themselves at home in our religious observances.

"In this perfect uniformity the world of the present day will see the *cor unum et anima una* (the one soul and one heart) of the Christians of the primitive Church. In it we will find our glory and our strength : *Vis unita fortior* (union makes strength)—our glory resulting from our unfailing fidelity to the traditional practices of the Church our mother ; our strength against all sects which can offer but the shameful spectacle of unceasing change.

"Moreover, this genuflection before the God of the tabernacle daily repeated millions of times all over the world, by all Catholic men, women, and children, will be a radical, unceasing, universal refutation of the radical, unceasing, universal negations of the Revolution. Why will not this grand Catholic adoration, this solemn observance of the first law of creation be blessed by God and become one of the preludes of that triumph so desired and so desirable in the Church ?" *

---

* Mgr. Gaume, " La Génuflexion au XIX. Siècle."

CHAPTER IV.

THE IRISH A MISSIONARY PEOPLE PAR EX-
CELLENCE—THEIR ZEAL IN PROPAGATING
THE FAITH.

BUT the faith of the Irish does not confine itself solely to the public manifestations before men, or private before God alone; it takes a further step which seems but a natural consequence.

The sun does not keep his beams for himself: he sends them forth in fructifying rays of light. Fire is invading in its nature; the soldier not only defends his country but seeks to extend its frontier. Of a like nature in truth is faith. When man has grown wan and pale with years over his books—when after long nights of study he suddenly in the silence of his vigils discovers the solution of a long and difficult problem, he bursts into the streets of the city, and, like a new Archimedes, triumphantly cries to the silent echoes, "I have found it! I have found it!" If man is thus an *apostle* by nature when he discovers a fragment of truth, what will he then be when he finds himself in possession of truth itself? What will be his zeal when he possesses that ardent light which cannot be concealed, that fire which the Word came on earth to enkindle in all men? Soldier of the *Faith*, will he not also seek to extend her dominions? Possessing God, the first of all blessings, will he remain the sterile possessor of God without seeking to communicate Him to his brethren? Will he keep to himself this mysterious treasure, the greatest wealth of time and eternity? Is not faith then invading in its nature?

This, therefore, is the second characteristic of the *Irish faith*. Nations, like individuals, have each a special vocation. The vocation of a people is no longer to extend its " frontiers to the prejudice of its neighbors; this was the glory of Pagan nations, of the Romans, the greatest of all. But what was this glory? Tears and bloodshed? It was suitable for races whom Christianity had not yet reached. The vocation of Christian peoples is to diffuse truth, to enlighten nations less advanced in the knowledge of God, to bear to them at the price of labor and the peril of death eternal blessings —Faith, Justice, Civilization." *

This is the special vocation of the Irish

---

* Lacordaire, 'Vocation de la nation Française."

people. It was prepared from its cradle for this noble mission. All Europe was plunged in the darkness of barbarism when under the influence of the ardent words of St. Patrick, that Gallo-Roman who went from our midst, the most celebrated cloisters opened their doors to the noblest children of Ireland. In a short time this blessed land was transformed into a new Thebaid. "Never had the West witnessed anything to equal these *Cenobite cities*, as they have been justly named, of Bangor, Clonfert, and Clonnard. Each contained three thousand Cenobites. The Thebaid reappeared in Ireland, and the West could no longer envy the East."

"During the three centuries which followed its conversion," says the same author,* "Ireland seems to have been but one vast monastery. There was no valley so remote, no forest so dense, no island so isolated, in the midst of lakes or by the shores of the steep western coast continually washed by the Atlantic, that did not serve as a retreat for Anchorites or Cenobites, of whom traces still are found in the rare and rude ruins of their narrow cells, meet habitations for these rude and hardy soldiers of toil and penance."

* Montalembert's "Monks of the West."

This army of religious devoted themselves with holy ardor to the cultivation of letters and poetry, to clearing the forests, to the education of youth, and to sacred psalmody. In these monasteries, whither the converted bards flocked in large numbers, the chants, according to the *naïve* testimony of an old author, became so sweet that the angels bent down from heaven to hear them.*

This is exactly what has given this people an instinctive and imperative desire to spread themselves abroad, to carry and diffuse the Faith in distant countries, to become truly a missionary people. Nothing in fact can better prepare souls for an apostolic life than the silence of retreat and the austerity of a cloister. Thus at the voice of St. Patrick, St. Columbanus, and their rude disciples, the Irish Cenobite tears himself from his cell and speeds to the most distant shores. He hastens to propagate the Gospel, to combat paganism—in a word, to win to faith and civilization the European nations, from Scotland and Northumberland to the banks of the Rhine and the Danube.

"The preponderance of the Irish race in the work of preaching and the conversion of pagan

---

* La Villemarqué, "Légende Celtique," p. 109.

or semi-Christian nations, particularly in the seventh century, is undeniable ; France, Switzerland, Belgium, Germany, owe her an immortal debt of gratitude. The law of Christ was enthusiastically adopted by this branch of the great family of Celtic nations known as Hibernians, Scots, or Gaels, and whose descendants and language have survived, even to the present day, in Ireland, the Highlands of Scotland, Wales, and Lower Brittany ; and when Celtic vitality seemed about to perish in Gaul and Great Britain, under the double pressure of Roman decadence and Germanic invasion, she stood out among all Christian races as the one most devoted to the Catholic faith, and most zealous for the propagation of the Gospel. . . . The intensity of the ardor for knowledge, and apostolic zeal enkindled by St. Patrick in Ireland, can hardly be appreciated but by the immense extent of the propagation of the Gospel by the Irish during six centuries. This monastic nation therefore became the *missionary nation par excellence.* While numbers flocked to Ireland to procure religious instruction, the Irish missionaries launched forth from their island and covered the lands and seas of the West. Untiring navigators, they landed on the most desert islands ; they overflowed the continent with their successive immigrations. Forgotten and unknown in their own country, we must seek their names in the early annals of all European nations, and find their relics under the altars where they were placed by the gratitude of a people converted by their patience, their courage, their indefatigable energy."* We still find them everywhere, particularly in America, consumed with the same zeal, the same ardor for the propagation of truth. This time Providence prepares them in a different manner for the continuation of their mission among modern nations. They come, not as formerly from the school of the cloister, but from the school of misfortune and sorrow; two great masters whose lessons teach much and are rapidly learned.

"The mission," says O'Connell, "of the Irish nation is to be upon the cross, and to suffer there for the *propagation of the Gospel.*"

An American bishop utters the same thought: "Providence keeps this faithful people in affliction that they may leave their country, and by their dispersion sow the seed of Christianity among distant nations."† And, in fact, a martyr people, more than all others, is destined to extend the reign of faith; for "heaven was separated from the earth, the

* Montalembert's "Monks of the West."
† The late Bishop Byrne of Little Rock.

cross has reunited them ; from the foot of the cross comes everything that leads to heaven." *

It was at the foot of the cross that the centurion chosen to guard the Saviour beheld the truth and confessed the divinity of Christ ; it was at the death of St. Stephen that the great St. Paul began to see the light of faith ; it was in assisting at the martyrdom of the early Christians that the pagans were converted in large numbers ; it is by the martyrdom of one people that other peoples are saved.

But in order to reach these people to be saved, it is necessary to overcome the difficulty of distance ; it is necessary to speak their language in order to communicate with them. God has provided for this.

For centuries there has been an intermingling of the Anglo-Saxon race and the Irish nation, at least a material and exterior fusion ; involuntary no doubt, and even forced, for it is in opposition to the character of the two peoples ; but circumstances and their mutual necessities compel it. Thus the force of circumstances has imposed the English language on Ireland to the extent of almost making the ancient Celtic language forgotten. The Irish, driven from their native soil by the miseries

* Lamennais.

resulting in a great part from British policy, have settled, owing to the fact that English in spite of themselves became their tongue, in countries where that language is spoken. Another determining cause attracts them to these countries: the development of commerce and industries due to Anglo-Saxon genius affords the Irish a means of sustenance.

Borne by the vessels of those who are the enemies of Catholicism and their own persecutors, they go to the English-speaking nations which have most need to return to the ancient faith of their ancestors, and in exchange for perishable material goods, they give them spiritual treasure which is immortal. They plant their faith in the colonies of Great Britain, and particularly in the great republic of America.

Therefore the actual progress of Catholicism in English-speaking countries is due to the labor of two races. The Anglo-Saxon element gives its language, its commerce, its factories, its ships; it is the vehicle, the unconscious material but providential instrument. The Irish is the moving spirit. By its grand spirit of faith it is the moral instrument of the great movement toward Catholicism. Without the concurrence of the Irish the action of Catholicism would have been slow and unimportant; but without the Anglo-Saxon element Irish proselytism would have been almost sterile in its effects for want of material support.

Then let her go her way, this proud Britannia, parading her flag and her ships on all seas; let her carry in her vessels to the four quarters of the globe, to her distant colonies, to the extremity of the two Americas, her opium which brutalizes, her alcohol which burns the body, her mutilated Bible which kills the soul, her minister of the Holy Gospel, with his wife and children, who establishes trading posts under the protection of a powerful consul, who indulges in commerce and sows heresy: she knows not that she bears with her in the Irish the most powerful antidote to all this! And Ireland is the *missionary people;* her vocation is to propagate the *Catholic faith.*

This zeal of the Irish for the conversion of their neighbor is found even among the simplest souls of the humblest and poorest ranks in life.

A learned and virtuous priest, Rev. Felix Varela, distinguished for the part he took in the increase of Catholicism in New York, said one day to the present pastor* of the French church of that city: "I confess that I have probably received a greater number of converts into the

---

* The late Father Lafont.

Church than any other priest, but I must acknowledge that these numerous conversions, in which I erroneously appear as the principal actor, were most frequently, not to say always, the work of the Irish, and particularly poor servant girls."

Hardly more than twenty-five years ago in New York, when people advertised for servants great care was taken to exclude Catholics. One day an advertisement of this kind appeared in one of the principal papers of that city. A poor young Irish girl presented herself at the address indicated, furnished with the customary references. As she was exhibiting her papers one after another to the mistress of the house, the latter suddenly said :

"But, first of all, are you or are you not a Catholic?"

"Certainly, ma'am, I'm a Catholic, thank God!" was the young girl's reply.

"Then you could not have read the advertisement I put in the paper," replied the lady. "I absolutely will not have a Catholic in my house."

"Yes, I read your advertisement," humbly answered the young girl ; "but what difference does it make, ma'am, whether I am a Catholic or not, if I am a good and honest servant and serve you faithfully. Try me, ma'am, and if you are not satisfied with me you can always send me away."

The lady made no reply to this wise and modest answer, but fixed her eyes on the young girl. Something in her simple and modest exterior attracted her and she said :

"Well, you may come and I will make the experiment."

For many weeks the poor girl was subjected to a good deal of persecution on the part of the family and the numerous servants of the house ; her religious practices were mocked and ridiculed in every way. But the young Christian's faith was invulnerable ; her patience was equal to all her trials. Some months passed in this way, when an epidemic of scarlet fever broke out in the city, and two of the children were taken with it. This was the signal for a general stampede among all the other servants. The Irish girl alone remained at her post with generous courageous fidelity ; she watched the sick children day and night, lavishing every attention upon them with the tenderness of a mother until they were completely cured.

A few years later a new misfortune fell upon the family : a sudden failure carried off their fortune, and everything had to be sold.

There was a small piece of old family furniture in the house which tender associations made very dear to the mother's heart. The young Irish girl knew this, and understood what it cost her mistress to part with it; therefore, though it brought a high price, she bought it out of her savings and placed it in the room of the mother of the family. When the lady returned, the first thing which met her eyes within the four naked walls was the cherished piece of furniture which she supposed she had seen for the last time.

"How is it possible this is still here?" she exclaimed, quite pale and trembling with emotion.

"Yes, ma'am," replied the young girl, "it will never leave here, it is yours. I bought it for the pleasure of giving it to you."

The heart of a woman, particularly of a mother, is moved with even less eloquence than this. Her eyes filled with tears and she fell upon the neck of her servant, saying:

"Oh, what a beautiful religion is yours! Your heroic devotion to my children overcame me, but to-day has finished your work. It is ended. I am resolved to embrace your religion. I will be a Catholic."

Ancient Rome decreed a laurel crown for the courageous mortal who saved the life of a Roman citizen. Think you God will not reserve in heaven a more beautiful, a richer, a more glorious, above all a more durable crown, since it is eternal, for one who at the price of similar sacrifices shall have saved not the body but the soul of a Christian ; even though the heroic soul to be crowned is only a poor servant girl ?

CHAPTER V.

ZEAL OF THE IRISH IN DEFENDING THEIR FAITH—ARCHBISHOP HUGHES.

HE Irish who know how to manifest and confess their faith, who know how to propagate it, know also how to defend it, and if need be die for it.

"How I love these good Bretons! Their valiant faith, their sublime indignation, their courageous protests against the wrongs of the Church and her Head, is an incomparable spectacle in this granite race. Brittany has indeed done wisely in preserving her customs, her manners, her ancient faith eternally young and living." *

When a young Irish lady, not many years since, writing her sister from Brittany paid this beautiful tribute to the Breton faith, she spoke unconsciously, perhaps, of one of the most striking characteristics of the faith of her own country. For it is truly there we find *in a granite race, the valiant faith, the sublime indignation,*

---

* "Letters of a Young Irishwoman to her Sister."

the courageous protests against the wrongs of the Church and her Head.

Under the episcopate of the predecessor of the present Cardinal Archbishop of New York, Archbishop Hughes, whose apostolic zeal contributed so powerfully to the progress of Catholicism in America, Protestants took alarm at this progress, which continued in spite of obstacles and difficulties of every kind. A number of fanatics had concerted together to fall upon the Catholic churches on a certain day, and after pillaging them, burn them to the ground, and thus arrest with one stroke the *extraordinary encroachments of Popery.* Happily a rumor of their purpose came to the ears of a few Irishmen, and rapidly spread through the city. A meeting was called, and shortly after a procession of ten thousand Irishmen marched in full day to the residence of the Archbishop. A deputation was sent to his Grace to ask in the name of the multitude what course was to be taken. The Archbishop was ill, but he was carried to his balcony, and addressed them in words which will be ever memorable in the history of the Church of America:

"My dear friends, you know and you understand that under circumstances as grave as the present I should not, I cannot give you a *sword*, but I give you a *buckler!* . . . Attack no one, respect the liberty of all; but if others respect not yours, if they attack you, defend yourselves, defend your God and His ministers, defend your churches which are His temples; fight, suffer, and at need die for your faith!"

The procession retired at these words, and for three days and three nights the ten Catholic churches of New York were each guarded by a thousand Irishmen, firmly awaiting the enemy. But they came not. The fanatics, alarmed at the resolute attitude of the defenders of the Faith, abandoned their project. This proved a decisive blow to fanaticism; from that day no attempt of any kind has ever been made to trouble the peace of consciences. The Catholic Church has not ceased to enjoy perfect liberty, and to increase and advance with giant strides, scattering on its way to nations as well as individuals the two great blessings, *life* and *light*, which she brought to the world, and for which humanity hungered and thirsted four thousand years.

If, in a grave case like the above, the Irish possessed not that *valiant faith which knows how to defend itself;* if, indifferent spectators, they had offered no resistance to the words and deeds of the enemy, who can say how grievous might have been the consequences of their inaction, not to say weakness? Who can fathom the depth of the abyss into which triumphant fanaticism might not have plunged the young Church of America for many years?

We complain in our day of the immense increase of evil, of the success of impiety everywhere triumphant and victorious. The most sacred rights are despised, the holiest duties trampled under foot; virtue and justice scorned and outraged; vice and injustice applauded and honored. Ah! the cause of this disorder, if we would know it, is that the good will not sustain the struggle; the strength of the wicked comes chiefly from the weakness of the good. The devil, they say, is a *lion and an ant* in combat—a *lion* for those who face him with the courage of an ant; an *ant* for those who face him with the courage of a lion.

The same may be said of the wicked, worthy sons of their father; they attack with the force of a lion or an ant according to the manner in which their enemy meets them; strong before the weak, weak before the strong. Catholics are accused of being intolerant. Nothing is less true. Their fault, not to say their crime, at times is being too apt to take the attitude of the ant before evil, when they should meet it like a lion.

Why is not the sun intolerant? When he

bursts like a giant on his course, and appears above our heads in a splendor of light, all shadows vanish, darkness disappears, mists are swept away, he alone remains, a majestic and all-powerful king enthroned in the highest firmament! Yet no one ever thinks of accusing the sun of intolerance.

Then let the just imitate the intolerance of the sun. Our faith, in the firmament of the intellect, is like the sun in the firmament of stars. She is *Light!* Hence when dark clouds of impiety, falsehood, hypocrisy appear before her, she has the power and the right to say to the darkness: "Vanish, and give place to light and truth!"

The day when the just shall have the courage to speak thus, many battles deemed irrevocably lost will be forever gained, for on that day shall begin the combat between the lion and the ant.

CHAPTER VI.

THE SIMPLE, TRUSTFUL FAITH OF THE IRISH—THEIR VENERATION AND RESPECT FOR HOLY THINGS—THEIR UNLIMITED CONFIDENCE IN THEIR PRIESTS AND THE SACRAMENTALS OF THE CHURCH.

THE *Irish faith*, while knowing how to propagate, and at need defend itself, has nevertheless preserved at the same time qualities more humble but no less precious; it still remains *simple* and *trustful*.

Who that has not the happiness of knowing them could comprehend their respect and veneration for holy things, their unlimited confidence in everything which is nearly or remotely connected with religion?

I mentioned earlier in the book their habitual custom of sprinkling themselves several times with holy water on leaving the church. I should have added that they are frequently seen to fill a small phial from the contents of the font and carry it away with them as a precious treasure. In fact holy water plays an important part in the devotion of the Irish; it is the object of their liveliest confidence and deepest respect.

One of my colleagues giving holy water one day to an Irishwoman poured it into a small bottle, and as he did so she held both her hands under the phial to catch any drop which might escape, while her little daughter, a child eight years old, knelt down and extended both her hands to prevent a drop from falling to the ground. At the *Asperges* on Sunday before mass it is always easy to recognize the Irish. When the priest passes near them they extend both hands toward him in the hope of catching a drop of the *precious water*. This *holy water* is an all-powerful arm with which the priest must be ever furnished when he goes to visit the sick among the Irish, for it is always their first and at times their most efficacious remedy. Upon one occasion a priest in New York went to visit an Irishman in the last extremity. While the spiritual physician was still present, a corporal physician arrived. After examining the patient the latter said rather bruskly, believing the dying man unconscious, "There is nothing for me to do here; it is a case of cholera. There is no hope. I am going."

The sick man raised himself with much effort

to a sitting position, and fixing his eyes on the doctor thus addressed him : " I have the cholera, you say ; I am gone ; there is no cure for me, and you are going away. Yes, go ; and I will have recourse to another physician who will not abandon me. Here is my physician, my remedy," he exclaimed ; and plunging his hand into a large holy water font which hung at the head of his bed, he washed his face with its contents several times, making a large sign of the cross.

The act of faith was immediately rewarded : the sick man was cured.

Men who understand not the things of God reproach the Irish with this unlimited confidence. The impious frequently deride it ; the indifferent and lukewarm greet it with a smile and shrug of the shoulders. For the true Christian it is sufficient to know that there is nothing of trifling value in the Church of God ; from the moment she approves the use of anything, its importance is conclusive. " The Church is a great sovereign ; she does not descend to vain details. Mistress of the truth, she neither practices nor countenances ridiculous superstitions. Spouse of the infinite Wisdom whose wisdom governs all wisdom, who can possess better knowledge of the visible and invisible world, as well as of their relations with each other.

For eighteen centuries her enemies have never found her at fault." *

Now the Church has blessed this water, it is one of the sacramentals which she constantly employs in her ceremonies. She attaches the greatest importance to it, judging by the prayers she repeats. In blessing holy water the exorcisms are uttered not in her own name, nor in the name of a vain and impotent idol, but in the name of God, who is light, life, and truth: *per Deum vivum, per Deum verum, per Deum sanctum.*† She asks several times that this water may procure for all who use it health of soul and body; that it may drive the demon from them and baffle all his snares; that it may preserve them from epidemic and plagues.

Moreover, this holy water, already commendable through the prayers of the Church and the use she makes of it in behalf of the faithful who are blessed with it from the cradle to the tomb, is no less commendable for several other reasons.

First of all, if antiquity is a claim for respect, what is there more noble than holy water whose origin is so ancient?

Moses, by a solemn command of God, blessed the water at the foot of Mount Sinai; and with

---

* Bishop Gaume, "L'Eau Bénite au XIX. Siècle," p. 262.
† By the living God, by the true God, by the holy God.

this water, mixed with the blood of victims, they sprinkled the children of Israel to sanctify them before delivering to them the Tables of the Law.

The synagogue also had its holy water for the purification of the children of Israel; it was composed of ordinary water mixed with the ashes of a heifer which had been burned as a victim. The use of it recurs continually in the prescriptions of the old law. Lepers, those who had carried the carcass or eaten the flesh of certain animals—in a word, all those who contracted any legal stain according to the Jewish law—were purified with this water.

Did not the pagans themselves have their lustral water which they used in their prayers and sacrifices? Thus counterfeiting the city of good by the city of evil, for the devil—that ape of God, as Tertullian says—is the great plagiarist of the Church. Protestants forget this in their ignorance or malice upon this point as well as many others, when they accuse the Catholic Church of having taken for her ceremonies the lustral water of pagans. Truth does not copy error; but error endeavors to clothe itself in truth, and thus disfigures it. The first Christians, particularly, used holy water constantly. St. Clement, the disciple and successor of St. Peter, attributes the formula of its benediction to St. Matthew the Apostle. Baronius proves that in the year 132 the people were sprinkled on Sundays. In the second century the pope St. Alexander, martyr and fifth successor of St. Peter, speaks of holy water as being universally used in the Church. "We bless this water mixed with salt," he says, "that by its aspersion all may be sanctified and purified, we order all priests to give this benediction."

The eloquence of illustrious facts and numerous records in the lives of saints of all periods of Christianity preach respect for holy water.

St. John Chrysostom restored to its weeping parents a child whom he brings back to life by sprinkling it three times with holy water in the name of the Holy Trinity. St. Germain, Bishop of Auxerre, in the midst of a terrible tempest, at the instance of his companions throws a few drops of holy water on the waves, and immediately He who arrests their fury with a grain of sand on the shore, arrests it again with a few drops of this water. St. Theresa, who frequently used it, says that she always, in moments of trial and particularly in visible attacks of the devil, experienced the difference between a simple sign of the cross and one made with holy water. "I have frequently experienced," she says, "that nothing equals the power of holy water in banishing the devils and preventing their return. . . . I am struck with the grand character which the Church imprints on all that she establishes. I tremble when I behold the mysterious strength which her words communicate to water, and the astonishing difference between that which is blessed and that which is unblessed."* In one of his voyages to England St. Malachy, Archbishop of Armagh in Ireland, who later became the companion of St. Bernard at Clairvaux, sprinkled a woman with holy water who was being consumed by a cancer; the pain ceased at once, and the next day no trace of the disease remained. St. Bernard, who relates this wonderful fact, was not behind his friend in miracles. By sprinkling with holy water he himself delivered several persons possessed of the devil, and restored innumerable sick to health.

I could continue to multiply instances. But why should it astonish us to see the same causes produce the same effects? The arm of God is not shortened.

But it is particularly in their intercourse with the priest that one sees, in all its beauty as

---

* " Life of St. Theresa."

well as in all its strength, the simplicity, the *naïveté*, and *confidence of the Irish faith.*

In Europe—thanks to the daily calumnies of an impious and irreligious press, which holds before the public rare and inevitable scandals; thanks also to the decay of a spirit of faith in the people—the priest no longer appears with that aureole of glory which Jesus Christ places on the head of all those whom he calls to the sublime mission of His eternal priesthood. Instead of proclaiming his salutary influence in the happiness of people and individuals, he is considered an enemy.

M. Cousin and M. Cochin were one day walking together in the court of the French Institute when a priest passed carrying on his arm a surplice and a stole. Cousin regarded him a moment and said to his colleague: "Do you see that young priest? He is about to do a great deed, for he is going to help a man to die well. For thirty years I have been speaking on the soul and its destinies, on man and his duties, but what results have I obtained? This priest has done more in one year than I in thirty. He has encouraged the young girl in virtue, the wife in fidelity; he has succored the poor, consoled the afflicted, raised hearts cast down by suffering or the treason of men; above all, he has aided his brother to die well.

Yes, in truth, I say to you this priest has done much more than all of us. And yet he is the man nevertheless whom they would banish from our midst ! . . . In vain I repeat they are the men truly needed, and we, with all our science, are useless !"

The Irish think with M. Cousin ; they are not, and never will be of the opinion of those who think the priest must be banished from their midst. The Irish, like the Christians of the early Church, behold the priest in all his greatness ; they see and salute in him, as in the epochs of faith, the friend, the confidant, the guide, the natural defender of the poor, the most faithful consoler of those who suffer. They know "that he is ready to brave and to suffer everything, to give baptism to the infants, catechism to the little children, the nuptial blessing to the young couple, divine bread for the last journey to the dying. And he is loved and respected for this devotion ; they venerate and cherish him. Wherever he presents himself he is recognized as the most loyal friend and protector of the family." *

If we insulted the sun, and the magnificent planet willed to avenge our insults, it would not be necessary that he should draw near to

---

* Bishop Mermillod.

consume us in his fire ; he need but withdraw from us, and he would find ample vengeance in the chaos, darkness, and night of his absence. It is the same with men when they insult the priesthood, and through it its Founder and divine Chief, the Priest *par excellence,* our Lord Jesus Christ. In the last days the Sun of Justice will appear ; He will draw near to His enemies to confound and overwhelm them. But meanwhile if He willed to take vengeance for the insolence of man, like the material sun, He need but withdraw His priesthood, and the darkness of death would follow.

The Irish understand this : therefore the ministry of the priest among them is most consoling, loved, and respected ; it powerfully influences them even in the most intimate domestic details. Among them the priest is truly the father of his flock. In fact this sweet name is the only one by which the Irish designate him ; he is not their pastor, but their *Father.*

Nothing is more touching, in the country and remote settlements and hamlets, than the arrival of the priest among his spiritual children, particularly at Christmas and Easter. It is at these periods that the priest makes his pastoral tour through the settlements and hamlets which compose his parish. He starts early in the morning and arrives about eight o'clock at the house which has the honor of being selected to serve as a chapel. There he finds all the families of the neighborhood assembled. He begins at once to hear confessions, and continues until noon. Then a piece of furniture is transformed into an altar and the indefatigable apostle celebrates mass. He gives holy Communion to these rude Christians, who kneel in turn before him, many of them coming from outside the cabin, which is too small to contain them all. After a thanksgiving made in common, he shares the frugal repast of his host; frequently a little bread and a few apples is the best fare the house can offer. The afternoon and evening are spent in administering the sacraments of baptism and matrimony, in catechising the children and visiting the sick. The next day, in the neighboring hamlet, the same ministry—that is, the same labor and the same consolations—until the whole parish has received the visit of *the Father*.

Happy family! A noble existence, a grand and glorious mission is that of this priest: poor, but free to do good!

Is there anything on earth more glorious before God, more useful to men, but at the same time more meritorious and more consoling for the apostle to such a people? "There, grace increases and the number of the faithful is daily multiplied; the Church flourishes with new vigor, its ancient and perfect beauty is renewed. There the faithful hasten to kiss the feet of the priest as he passes; they carefully gather with eager and hungry hearts the least portion of God's Word which falls from his lips. During all the week they await with impatience the day of the Lord, when, united as brothers in a holy rest, they exchange the kiss of peace, being but one heart and one soul. They sigh for the joys of their assemblies, for the chants and praises of the Lord, for the sacred feast of the Lamb. One could believe he was witnessing the labors, the journeys, the dangers of the Apostles with the fervor of the *infant churches.*"*

If Fénelon could have witnessed the faith and fervor of the Irish, he could not have depicted it better than he does in the vivid picture which he gives of the infant churches. It is not only in the silent little country hamlets that this consoling spectacle is found, but in the midst of the noisiest and busiest cities of the American Union. For there, in fact, we always find the same respect, the same veneration for the priest, and the same unlimited confidence in him; their respect for the priest

---

* Fénelon, "Sermon sur l'Epiphanie."

and their confidence in him resemble in a measure that which they feel toward God.

You will not meet a priest who has spent some months in America that has not from time to time had an Irishman or an Irishwoman come to him and say, kneeling before him, "Father, I am sick. Will you cure me?" If the priest answers, "How can I cure you? I am not a doctor," the patient will immediately answer, "No, father, you are not a doctor, but neither were the Apostles; you are one of their successors, you are a priest like them, you can do what they did; give me your blessing and I will be cured." In vain the priest may add, "But I cannot work miracles, for I am not a saint like the Apostles." All the same he must give his blessing. And, in fact, many times this strong and at the same time simple confidence is rewarded here below: the miracle solicited is granted. Is it not to faith like this that the Master has solemnly promised the power of moving mountains?

How many instances I have seen of that faith equally touching and simple!

One day I saw at the sacristy door a good old Irishwoman whom I judged by her wrinkled countenance and mouth innocent of teeth to be about eighty years of age. She was sick and had come to be cured. While explaining the object of her visit she handed me a small bottle, which I knew meant—fill it with holy water. I passed into the adjoining room, and was absent long enough to comply with her silent request. On my return imagine my astonishment to see the good woman barefooted and to hear her say, "Father, my feet are sore; touch them, make the sign of the cross over them, and I will be cured." There was no refusing her request, and I had to follow exactly, point for point, the ceremonial she indicated. This done, the octogenarian resumed her shoes and stockings and started for home with a light step. I never saw her again. Did I at least once in my life enjoy the privilege of a thaumaturgos?* I cannot say. But the simple faith of the good woman was truly worthy of reward.

The second week of my stay in New York I found myself one day in a church in an Irish part of the city. There was very little in my dress to indicate that I was a priest. Nevertheless a poor woman respectfully approached the place where I was kneeling, and after regarding me attentively murmured something in my ear of which—thanks to English abbreviations and only half-caught words, as well as my ignorance of the language—I comprehended

* Wonder-worker.

not a word except that she was speaking of a cross. I replied as best I could, using abbreviations in my turn, "I *don't speak English.*" My interlocutor insisted, repeated her phrase, and I mine, which about composed my repertoire of English at that time. Finally, resolving not to be defeated, she seized my hand, and taking possession of my thumb made the sign of the cross with it on her forehead. It was an Irishwoman who had recognized me as a Catholic priest, and wanted my blessing.

Upon another occasion in New York, an Irishwoman fell on her knees before me in the open street and said, "Please give me your blessing."

At Montreal, Canada, in the month of December, 1869, I had new proof of the depth of the pious attachment of the Irish for the priest.

A Sulpitian father employed in the parish of an Irish church died suddenly. For two days there was an unceasing procession, which was most touching ; twenty thousand Irish succeeded one another without interruption in the room where the dead priest lay, all praying and weeping as if they had lost a father or mother. On the day of the funeral twelve thousand Irish would accompany the remains to the cemetery, though there was four feet of snow on the ground ; the cold was intense, the thermometer that day being thirty degrees below zero.

About the end of the year 1870 I went once or twice a week to say mass at the "Little Sisters of the Poor," who had just been established in New York. After the mass was ended the Irish men and women always went forward before leaving the chapel, and bent the knee before the altar, then turning toward the priest never failed to salute him, and also the religious, if any of them were still in the chapel. The superior of the house said to me one day: "We can absolutely do whatever we please with these good old Irish people; they are like little children with us. Their respect for religious is something admirable; a word from us is like an oracle from heaven to them."

I lived seven years in New York the companion of a holy French priest who at the time of the Civil War was stationed in St. Augustine, Florida. A regiment of Irish soldiers encamped near Charleston asked for him, and my friend, heeding only his zeal, started at once despite the great distance between the two cities. On arriving he threw himself into the first tent he came to and began hearing confessions.

The colonel, a Protestant, informed of his arrival, came to him at once.

"Father," he said, "I cannot allow you to

remain in here so ill accommodated. My tent is at your disposal for the time that you are among us. Permit me to install you at once."

"But, colonel, you forget," replied the priest, "my ministry here may be prolonged for some time. I will be at work all day and perhaps far into the night; therefore I cannot accept your kind offer. I cannot consent to thus turn you out of your quarters."

"But I insist upon it, Father, this is no place for you. Come."

The missionary could not but yield. He occupied the colonel's tent, not for a few days or a few weeks, but for three entire months.

When the colonel reviewed the regiment, he always had the chaplain beside him on horseback, in his cassock. Toward the end of his stay in the Irish camp the colonel said to him, at one of the grand reviews:

"Father, behold my brave Irishmen! What good faces they have! They are fine soldiers!"

"Colonel," replied the priest, "they are also my children in a measure, and I share your pride in them."

"Father, you truly have reason to do so. I must acknowledge that during the three months that you have been among us they are indebted to you for many of the virtues for which they are distinguished, and which make them doubly dear to me."

Here, then, is a people who do not fear the influence of a military chaplain. There at least they are not too blind or too malicious to understand that he who preaches the service of God preaches at the same time devotion to country. In the words of Bossuet, "Whoever loves not God, whatever he says, whatever he promises, truly loves but himself."

Delicacy is also another characteristic of their simple faith. This is particularly apparent in their manner of expressing their gratitude. The manner of bestowing a gift, whatever it may be, always increases or diminishes its value. Being gracefully grateful doubles the gratitude. The gratitude of the Irish toward their pastor is most gracefully manifested.

When a missionary for a certain number of years devotes himself to the rude labors of the apostolate in a foreign clime, it not unfrequently happens that his courage outlives his strength, and he is obliged to return to his native country to recover strength for renewed labors. It is upon such an occasion that the tender attachment of the Irish for their pastor and the delicacy and charm of their gratitude is most striking. They never allow him to take his departure until every effort has been made to secure him every comfort for his long voyage. A subscription is taken up, and a few days before his departure the sum collected is offered to the beloved pastor with the greatest delicacy. At New York and other seaport towns the scene is still more touching. A deputation from the parish accompanies the priest to the steamer, and there, while wishing him, on the part of all his flock, a pleasant voyage, their generous offering is delivered to him. Sometimes the missionary is never to return, and the emotion and tears visible in every countenance involuntarily recall the parting between Paul and the Milesians. The same scene is veritably reproduced. "*And there was much weeping among them all; and falling on the neck of Paul they kissed him, being grieved most of all for the word which he had said that they should see his face no more. And they brought him on his way to the ship*" (Acts 20 : 37, 38).

When the missionary is to return, he does not draw largely for his comforts from the generous offering of his flock. Nevertheless, though his whole baggage on leaving consisted of one small trunk, on his return it is astonishingly increased by the addition of several enormous boxes. The money of his good Irish people, destined to procure him comforts on his journey, has been converted for the most part into church ornaments of every kind for the church, not unfrequently the churches, of which he has charge—candelabra, chalices, stations of the cross, statues, etc. Indeed it was a struggle between delicacy and generosity on both sides.

A French priest, while pastor of an Irish church near Chicago, attained the twenty-fifth anniversary of his priesthood. His faithful parishioners, wishing to celebrate his silver jubilee, had recourse to an innocent ruse which shows their sincere devotion, their respectful gratitude, and a multitude of other sentiments no less worthy of admiration in a flock toward their pastor, in children toward a *father*. The day before the long-expected anniversary it was so arranged that the pastor was absent for twenty-four hours from his home. On his return the following day, what was his astonishment as he alighted from the car to see his whole parish at the depot to meet him! As soon as he appeared in sight a band struck up a joyous air, the people carrying flags and banners fell into a line of march, and a long procession escorted him to the rectory, where new and touching surprises prepared by his grateful flock awaited him. Twenty-four hours had been sufficient to effect a complete transformation in his house. All the old furniture had disappeared as if by magic, and was replaced by a handsome new set. On the étagère one of the principal pieces was a valuable vase which held an exquisite bouquet of flowers. This graceful and poetic expression of sympathy and congratulation came from the good Father's absent sister in France. On its arrival it was adroitly turned from its first address and retained as a double and pleasing surprise for the worthy pastor on this day.

What is there more touching and more beautiful in the life of a people than this holy respect for religious authority, than these fraternal relations between those who command and those who obey, than these pious and delicate manifestations of gratitude, than this charming, simple testimony of loving hearts?

What a contrast between this and the ignoble scenes which have recently been enacted in France! Who does not still remember that false preacher of Meudon hunting down the seminarists of foreign missions? Who can forget the scene presented by a mad populace pursuing two inoffensive priests with hootings and menaces through the streets of Paris, ready to drown them any moment? And of what crime were they guilty? Ah! an impious press had roused this multitude; it had signally calumniated these priests to the people, representing them as the sole cause of all their misfortunes in that cry which has become so sadly famous, "Clericalism! Behold the enemy!"

CHAPTER VII.

STRENGTH OF THE IRISH FAITH AT THE HOUR OF DEATH—ZEAL OF THE IRISH FOR THE REPUTATION OF THE CLERGY.

T is when the Irish are face to face with death that one sees the greatness and depth of their almost unlimited confidence in the father and director of their soul. A word from his lips is frequently life or death to them. I would not venture to assert this had I not witnessed it myself, extraordinary as it may appear.

I had many proofs of it in the August of 1876, when the temperature of New York was like that of the torrid zone. Nothing like the heat had been experienced for sixty years. The thermometer was 98° at midnight, and the air was stifling. For a whole week the people passed the nights on the roofs of the houses, in the open squares, and even on the sidewalks. They were literally dying of heat. Woe to those who imprudently exposed themselves to the heat of the sun! There were from eighty to a hundred sunstrokes a day.

One of these terrible nights I was called to the bedside of an Irishman who was dying, I was told, in one of the principal hotels of the city. "Father," he exclaimed, as soon as I appeared, "hear my confession at once, and give me Extreme Unction, for I feel that I am going to die."

"No, you are not," I immediately answered; "you are not so low; you will not die."

He regarded me with astonishment for a moment, and then said:

"Do you really, conscientiously think so, Father? Are you really earnest?"

"To show you that I really think so, I am going to leave you now without hearing your confession or giving you the last sacraments."

He looked at me for a moment, and the whole expression of the sick man's face changed. However, as he urged me to hear his confession, I did so, telling him several times that confession, whether in health or sickness, was always salutary. The next morning I brought him Holy Communion, and three days after he was up.

During that week I had occasion to exercise my ministry in behalf of more than a dozen Irish people suffering from a similar attack, and they all, without exception, recovered in the same remarkable manner through the influence of the same means.

Here is a still more significant occurrence of a similar kind, which was witnessed about the same time in a family of my acquaintance living near New York.

A young Irishwoman, a fervent Catholic, the mother of a numerous family and the wife of a Frenchman, was on her deathbed. The doctor, after one of his visits, convinced that there was no hope for his patient, was despondently turning over her case in his mind when suddenly a bright thought occurred to him. He retraced his steps and went to a Catholic college near by, and said to the superior :

"Father, your neighbor is dying. I have vainly exhausted all the resources of my profession. You are her spiritual director ; as a priest, confessor particularly, you possess an influence over her which I as her physician cannot claim. Tell her very decidedly that she must live for her family. If you firmly insist, I am sure she will live.

A moment after, the priest was at the bedside of the dying woman.

"Well, my child," he said, "how are you getting on to-day?"

"Oh, Father!" she replied, with a smile, "I know perfectly well I have only a few days, perhaps a few hours to live ; nevertheless I am happy to die, since it is God's holy will to take me. My only regret," she continued, joining her hands and raising her eyes to heaven, " is leaving my children. It is always hard for a mother to leave them, particularly the youngest ; but I confide them to God's care, and I will watch over them from heaven."

"No, no," replied the priest, " it is not from heaven you must watch over your children, but here upon earth ; you must continue the work of a mother which God has given you by remaining in their midst to complete their Christian education already so well begun. This is God's will for you. Promise me that you are going to do everything that depends upon you to get well."

"You think then that is God's will, Father?"

"Yes, I am certain it is."

"And you insist that I must think only of getting well?"

"It is your duty as a mother."

"Then I promise it."

She recovered.

If this fact seem to some exaggerated, it is perhaps the occasion to recall the conduct of another physician, one of our modern celebrities. The celebrated savant called to the bedside of a young man whose days seemed numbered, though possessed of very little piety himself, began by advising immediate recourse to the succors of religion, particularly confession. When asked by his friends the reason of his strange prescription the physician replied: "The aids of religion in general, particularly confession, quiet the soul in a marvellous manner; the soul once tranquil and at peace, remedies act much more efficaciously; it is by curing the soul that we cure the body."

Protestant physicians themselves have, with great liberality and frankness, made the same remark. Dr. Tissot relates that at Lausanne he was called to a rich young heir whom he found in a state of the most violent agitation. Terrible were the transports of his despair at the thought of leaving all his possessions and his brilliant future. "I know but one thing that will cure you," said the doctor to him: "send for a priest and make your confession!" He did so, and the following day alarming symptoms disappeared, calmness was restored, and the dying man was brought back to life.

The Protestant doctor was fond of relating this incident. He was too just to be afraid to add: "What a powerful thing, then, is confession! It restores to peace of soul one who is dying in despair, and the moral cure effects the physical."

This *Irish faith*, which so truly appreciates religious practices, which carries its respect and veneration for the ministers of Jesus Christ to so high a degree, seems at times to be inspired with the sentiments of the great Constantine. "If I had the misfortune to see a priest fall," says the illustrious emperor, "I would hasten to cover his fault with my royal mantle that none might be scandalized."

Under the episcopate of Bishop Dubois of New York a certain number of Irish embarked for America. On board was a priest from their own country, but during the passage his conduct gave very little edification. As they neared port they perceived that their compatriot, doubtless with the idea of celebrating their fortunate passage and saluting the new country, had quite forgotten himself. His condition was such that he could not appear without much discredit to his calling and his country, and scandal to the public. They held a council among themselves, and after mature deliberation unanimously resolved to send back to the old country this degenerate representative of the priesthood, so little worthy of Ireland and his noble mission. Each one drew out his purse and the sum necessary for a return passage was soon collected. Alongside of their vessel was another just preparing to weigh anchor and sail direct to Queenstown. The unfortunate man was passed on board with his baggage, and a few moments afterward, wholly unconscious that he had reached port, was venturing anew the perils of the high seas, profoundly wrapped in the arms of Morpheus. Judge what must have been his awakening! Soon, however, a serious remorse took possession of the consciences of the good Irish people who had so promptly returned the apostle to his mother country. Had they not, they asked themselves, incurred a penalty of excommunication or anathema of some sort by dealing so summarily with a priest? To solve the embarrassing problem what was to be done? The most skilful casuists among them decided that there was but one thing—to have recourse to authority. A deputation was at once selected to proceed to the residence of Bishop Dubois and lay the case before him. Imagine their surprise when the bishop, after a hearty laugh, said : "' My dear friends, so far from having incurred any anathema, I owe you a special blessing for the good deed you have performed." They knelt down, and the bishop, still smiling, gave them his benediction. This is how a people who have preserved the simplicity of the faith conduct themselves.

In France, since she has become more

learned and less Christian, since she has attained more wealth and less faith, the conduct of her children rarely resembles this. When, from time to time a scandal appears, the single event is made a general one; all are absolutely held responsible for the fault of an individual. Could anything be less reasonable, to say the least?

What! Did not Jesus Christ Himself choose His apostles? Did He not seek them from one end of Judea to the other? On the borders of the lake He chose twelve poor, simple, ignorant men of the people, in whom the passions are weaker. He Himself determined the choice of them, and among these twelve was found a traitor; among twelve priests one unfaithful one! What a lesson for the world! There are 50,000 priests in France, and the corrupt and corrupting world is appalled at the defection of one of that number. And when a priest abandons Jesus Christ, rends his sacerdotal robe, proves false to his mission, and places himself under the world's flag, the malice of the world calumniously fastens the fault of the individual upon the whole order. There was a traitor in the apostolic college, but it does not follow that all were traitors, since they proved with their life, their blood, their martyrdom, the fidelity which they had vowed to their Master. Therefore, when a priest falls, O world ! the Church has condemned him before thee. If he present himself to thee it is because the Church has cast him forth. She rejects him from her bosom. Whether he is called Lamennais, or signs himself Hyacinthe, she abandons him to thee. He is worthy henceforth to walk under thy banner, for he is thy imitator, he is one of thine ; we give him to thee. But thy crime is choosing this occasion to deride on the boards of a licentious stage, to calumniate in the caricatures of illustrated journals given as food to the intelligence of the people, to daily exhibit in the pillory of thy infamous journals the French Catholic priesthood, which so nobly bears unspotted on its brow the triple crown of chastity, patriotism, and devotion.

CHAPTER VIII.

GENEROSITY OF THE IRISH FAITH—THE NEW CATHEDRAL OF NEW YORK — EXTRACTS FROM THE "LETTERS OF A YOUNG IRISHWOMAN TO HER SISTER."

COULD I forget to say a word now of the *generosity of the Irish faith?*

No obstacle deters it; it stops at no sacrifices, whatever their nature, *material* or *moral*.

Under this double point of view I scarcely know what traits to choose in illustration, so numerous and edifying are those which press into my memory as I write. It is from the purse of the Irish that the churches, Catholic schools, rectories, and hospitals are built and maintained. It is no exaggeration to say that in America generally, particularly New York, two thirds of the Catholic churches are erected by the *generosity of the Irish.* "They build churches," says an American bishop,* "before they think of building handsome houses

---

* Bishop Lynch.

for themselves." Their motto is: *The house of God before everything.*

No sooner are a few Irish cabins grouped together, no sooner have the brave people conquered to civilization a few acres of land in the forest or the plains, than they build a church and a school beside it. The house of the Lord rises in the midst of the lowest hamlet and peacefully shadows the home of the pioneer. We find the church in the midst of the plains, in the mountain gorges ; she protects the husbandry of the farmer, and the labor of the miner whose village hangs like an eagle's nest on the side of the rocks in Colorado." *

When American Catholics build a church, after the first foundation is laid they always have an imposing ceremony, which is called *laying the corner stone.* In the cities the bishop presides and the crowd is very great. Temperance societies, Confraternities, Irish associations with banners flying, accompanied by a band of music, march in procession to the ceremony. A long and imposing service is followed by a sermon in the open air, the procession defiles before the corner stone, each one as he passes leaving a liberal offering. An Irishman does not consider a large sum of

* Yonveaux, " L'Amérique Actuelle."

money offered on this day any sacrifice, but rather an honor. He is proud and happy to contribute to the erection of God's house, and thus assist and further the progress of his faith. It rarely happens that the amount collected on that day is not sufficient to send up the walls to the dome.

On the 25th of May, 1879, thirty-six American prelates, archbishops and bishops, and many thousand privileged witnesses assisted at the consecration of the new St. Patrick's Cathedral of New York, begun twenty years before by Bishop Hughes, then archbishop of that city. This was certainly one of the most imposing ceremonies ever witnessed in the New World, and it is probable that the present generation will never see anything like it. Veritable triumph—not only in a religious point of view, but also in art and architecture, it was a visible sign, an incontestable proof of the incomparable development of Catholicism during the later years. Since 1810 it has increased seven times more than all the other religious denominations put together, and for the last ten years the increase has been doubled.

The new cathedral is a beautiful edifice in white marble, in the Gothic of the thirteenth century, the only fault of which is that it is too ornamental; for the rest it is rich and graceful. The building covers 38,500 square feet of land, and seats 2500 persons, with standing room for 4000. The total length of the interior is 306 feet, its width 96 feet; the length of the transept is 140 feet, and the height to the dome is 108 feet.

The interior of the building, when completed, will have cost $4,500,000, and to finish the exterior a new outlay of $1,000,000 will be necessary. The main entrance is fifty-one feet high and thirty in width. Above it are beautiful carvings, with a row of niches destined for the statues of saints. The whole is surmounted by a rose window 26 feet in diameter.

The building is lighted by 70 superb windows, executed in France. On the right and left of the building are uniform chapels measuring 14 feet in width and 18 feet high. Until to-day the cathedrals of Mexico, Montreal, and Puebla were without a rival on the continent of America. St. Patrick's of New York will in future be the vastest and most beautiful edifice on that side of the Atlantic; it may even rival certain celebrated cathedrals of Europe. It is called, and not without reason, the New York Catholics' *tower of strength*. It was erected by the piety of the faithful, and chiefly by the humblest and poorest, without any assistance whatever from government authorities. But without being in the secrets of God we can affirm that the most beautiful blocks of marble in the edifice were paid for by the generosity of the Irish. Cardinal McCloskey, the present Archbishop of New York, tells of receiving a visit from two simple Irish servant girls, who each offered him for the new cathedral $200, the fruit of several years' saving.

The altar alone, which came from Italy, and is made of the most beautiful marbles to be found there, cost about $30,000; it is one of the richest in the world.

All this is the result of the offerings of the poor, of the savings of the Irish servant girl, and the economy of the laborer. As in the early ages the churches thus built are the property of all, the glory and the palace of those who possess none. What henceforth will Trinity Church, the metropolis of Protestantism (possessing by itself land estimated at $10,000,000) be beside the Catholic basilica built with the offerings of the poor.

To be just, however, we must say that generous offerings from the rich were added to those of the poor. At the beginning of the winter of 1875 the Archbishop of New York invited a hundred gentlemen to a lunch, telling them he had an important communication to make to them. At the end of the meal the archbishop rose and said :

"Gentlemen, I have assembled you here to day to tell you of the embarrassing strait in which I find myself. . . . You understand that we have undertaken a great work which, cost what it may, must be completed—that is, the building of our new cathedral. Now no later than yesterday the architect came to tell me that it could not be left unroofed this winter without serious damage to the edifice. . . . But, gentlemen, to take this great step in our enterprise will cost $100,000, and I have nothing."

A moment of silence followed the archbishop's words ; they glanced inquiringly at one another ; then, after a few words of consultation, each one wrote a check for $1000, and twenty-four hours after the laborers were at work. Among the generous donors this time there were not only Irishmen, but Frenchmen, Canadians whom I could mention, Americans, and even American Protestants.

If you would have a further proof of the marvellous generosity of the Irish on a smaller scale, visit the greater number of the parochial churches in the city of New York. Here is a large one which extends from street to street, and on either side of it rise two large buildings ;

they are schools for boys and girls; and a little further on is the priest's residence. What has paid, or rather what will pay for all this? *The generosity of the Irish.*

Get on board one of those commodious steamers which leave every few moments for some place near New York. You will soon be transported on the Hudson River to Yonkers. There the priest will be happy to show you his church, a magnificent hospital, and excellent schools kept by Christian Brothers and religious. Ask him how he found means to accomplish these great works in twenty years. He will answer: *I am the pastor of an Irish congregation.*

Let us continue our little journey. But twenty minutes more and you will find yourself in Jersey City! There again you will meet a French priest proud to show you a church, a rectory, schools, a hospital for the sick, an asylum for the poor, and another for the orphans. Ask him what munificent source furnished means for all these? He will give you the same reply: *The generosity of the Irish.*

Let us take the cars now to Newark, a city of 100,000 inhabitants, about six miles from New York. Another French priest, in *sabots*, his head protected by a straw hat, stands compass in hand in the midst of the masons, filling the *rôle* of architect from morning until night, with scarcely time for his meals. He has built one of the most beautiful churches in America; he was the sole architect; he drew the plans and directed all the work; he superintended the placing of every stone in the building. It is a veritable monument which people come from a distance to see. When I visited the indefatigable missionary, he was building in the rear of his church an immense stone hospital, and an iron school-house two hundred feet square, not far distant. Who placed in his hands the money which in the New World as well as the Old is indispensable for works of this kind? The answer is easily divined. He is pastor of an Irish congregation, and the money was the generous offerings of his parishioners.

This *generosity* is made a crime in the Irish: they are accused of being *extravagant, careless,* and *improvident.*

This improvidence for the things here below, if it is really a characteristic of the people, gives birth to so many noble qualities that I have not the courage to reproach them therewith.

Improvident! But at the present day, when we hear of nothing but loans and investments, the Irish, persuaded that in seeking first the kingdom of God all things shall be added unto them, could not better employ their money than by giving it to God and investing it in eternal treasure. Certainly they have no reason to fear pecuniary disasters; their interest is very high, their fortune is secured.

"Wealth is a gift of which we profit only by parting with it, which benefits man only in proportion as he distributes it, and it is by depriving himself of it that he makes a proper use of it." *

Those who comprehend this truth are not possessed by their riches, as a pagan philosopher has said, but truly possess their wealth; they are masters and proprietors of it, not slaves to it, but free to expend it in good works, to make to themselves, with the perishable treasure of a day, other treasure more real, more true—in a word, imperishable and eternal. Can this, then, be called a crime, extravagance, improvidence?

I should rather say it was the proper use of wealth, for employed according to the divine plan it can give wings to the soul in the path to heaven. It may even become one of the most efficacious means of sanctity, for in every good work the Christian imitates our Saviour in what may be called the noblest and dearest

* Bishop Bouillerie.

of all His divine attributes—mercy and goodness. Thus the first and most beautiful of virtues blossom and grow with wealth, and they call upon its assistance.

"Give me gold," cries *Faith*, "and I will convert it into grand basilicas where the people shall come to adore their Creator. I will convert it into lofty towers and sculptured spires which, rising to heaven, will announce afar the glory of the thrice holy God. Give me gold, and I will take my apostles, my missionaries, and send them beyond the seas, and those who sleep in the darkness and shadow of death will at last hear the good tidings; the little ones of China will be wrested from the teeth of animals, and made through baptism heirs to a heavenly inheritance."

"Give me gold," cries *Hope*, "and with the perishable treasure I will amass eternal treasure which neither the rust nor the moth doth consume. I will fly to heaven and there build myself an immortal and eternal dwelling."

"Give me gold," cries *Charity*, "and with it I will dry the tears of those who mourn, will feed the hungry, clothe the naked; I will give parents to the orphan; I will gather the aged and infirm ungratefully turned into the street, and give them '*Little Sisters of the Poor*'; I will erect hospitals for the sick. Give me gold, and if I do not cause all the miseries of the world to disappear, I will at least alleviate a great many."

It is because the Irish lend an attentive ear to the sublime teachings of these three daughters of God—Faith, Hope, and Charity, that they are prodigal of their gold. Can we consider their *generosity* a crime? On the contrary, is not their almost natural love of *material sacrifice* most honorable to them? They will never be exposed to the remorse of which the poet sings : .

> " Moi-même, plein des biens dont l'opulence abonde,
>   Que j'échangerais volontiers
> Cet or dont la fortune avec dédain m'inonde,
>   Pour une heure du temps ou je n'avais au monde
>   Que ma vigne et mon figuier !
> Pour ces songes divins qui chantaient en mon âme
>   Et que nul or ne peut payer." *

> And I whom Fortune, with a calm disdain,
>   O'erwhelms with golden opulence, would give
> All that she lavishes could I regain
>   One sunny hour of the dead past and live
> As in the days when I possessed no more
> Than vine and fig-tree by the cottage-door,
> And hear again the sacred songs of truth—
> Those priceless echoes of my sinless youth.

Side by side with *material sacrifice* is another

---

* Lamartine.

far higher and more difficult—*moral sacrifice*, which the Irish meet with no less courage.

In an age of moral corruption, when soul and conscience are bartered for gold, when the greater number bow down before brute force or triumphant success, it is beautiful to hear the Irish, with the faith of early days, repeat the ancient motto which was graven on the hearts as well as on the escutcheons of our ancestors : *Potius mori quam fœdari!* (Death before dishonor!)

When, in fact, to preserve the treasure of their faith there is question of moral sacrifice, often so bitter, the Irish never hesitate for a moment.

Who has not heard the history of the poor Irish farmer, the father of a family in prison for debt? A lord, his creditor, in cruel kindness had set him free on condition that he should vote against O'Connell.

The price of the vote to the unfortunate man was freedom, the assurance of daily food to his starving family, a return to his home, to his aged mother, his wife, his children. He advanced to the ballot-box with hesitating steps and anxious brow, tears of shame almost blinding him. On one side he saw, not only for himself but his family, destitution, with its terrible train of attendant evils ; on the other, his country in chains, her Liberator betrayed. What must be his choice? Love for his own triumphed, and seizing the abhorred ticket with a feverish hand he frantically rushed toward the box, when a lean hand was placed on his arm and a voice screamed in his ear:

"What are you doing, unfortunate man? Remember your soul and your liberty!"

It was his poor old mother who thus recalled him to his duty and his honor.

The noble words of the poor woman transformed the heart of the son, father, and husband. With a lofty mien he proudly tore the dishonoring paper and flung the name of O'Connell into the ballot-box; then returned with a firm step to his prison. He doubtless resumed his chains; but his heart was comforted and his conscience was at peace. He had not betrayed his country; he had *been mindful of his soul and liberty!*

This woman—this Christian, this heroic mother—is a true, living, and noble type of the Irish, who, by the union of their faith and their patriotism, *sacrifice everything to God, their religion and their country.*

A poor Irishwoman living in New York was left a widow with four children, the oldest of whom had only just attained his seventh year. Fervent Christian and devoted to her family, this was her daily prayer: "Lord, if my children are not to remain good Christians; if one day they must lose their innocence, their only treasure here below; if one day they shall offend Thee by mortal sin, I beg of Thee to take them out of this world while they are still in Thy holy grace."

The prayer of this new Blanche of Castile was heard: to-day her four children are in heaven. Many doubtless will not understand this. And yet this is a truly Christian mother! With her the soul is before the body, heaven before earth, eternity before time. One day this woman of generous faith will leave this earth and she will behold her four children coming to meet her, radiant and transfigured with the glory of Christ. In this embrace, this reunion which will never end, she will see why God heard her prayer, why He separated her from her children; then she will comprehend how the sorrow of a day has purchased for them all the incomparable happiness of living during all eternity reunited in the same light, the same happiness, the same love. What admirable doctrine! It was also well understood by that young Irish exile who, writing to her sister from France, terminates her letter in these noble words: "*Au revoir*, dear Kate; may God protect us! When shall I see Ireland again? When shall I again see the soil from which my ancestors were banished—my ancestors, sons of a royal race? *Faith is better than a throne.*" *

Toward the end of September, 1870, in New York, a policeman was stabbed by a drunkard in the street and seriously wounded. A priest was sent for in all haste, and arrived at the same time with two physicians. "Gentlemen," said the wounded man, addressing the latter, "will you withdraw for a moment? The needs of my soul are more urgent than those of my body—my *soul* first of all, then my body." During his convalescence the priest who had attended him had given him "The Passion of Our Lord," by Catherine Emmerich, to read. The confessor at each visit exhorted him to patience, and he invariably replied: "Ah! how can any one complain of his sufferings who has read the book you lent me? How can I let a day pass without thinking of the sufferings of our Saviour, after I have gone through its holy pages."

It is this same generosity of the Irish which inspires in them at times noble words worthy of the first Christians, which merit to be graven in characters of gold. Witness an old man

---

* "Letters of a Young Irishwoman to her Sister."

eighty years of age, and his wife sixty-four, driven from their cabin—a tottering ruin.

"Alas!" cried the poor woman, "here I am at my age without a shelter in the world; I who have never injured any one, but have always, when I could, given shelter to the poor and the unfortunate! What have I done to merit such a punishment?"

"Hush, woman," replied the old man, "the passion of our Lord was worse than this."

Here again, under a similar trial, are words equally grand.

An Irishman refused to leave his cabin, which the constable had come to tear down. It was all he had; it was his home, where he hoped to live and die. He was forcibly ejected, and as he stood a prisoner, watching the destruction of the poor hovel, his wife exclaimed, "Thank God! they cannot turn us out of heaven."

But it is particularly at the moment of the last supreme sacrifice, when face to face with death, that the *generosity of the Irish faith* appears in all its splendor. Then it rises to incomparable heights, and recalls all that is most sublime in the beautiful ages of the Church.

For death is a great revelation; it manifests the nature of souls much more truly than their words and acts during life. In the words of Bossuet: "It brings truth in its train." At this decisive moment the anxieties of life disappear, the noise of the world is silenced, illusions vanish, the veil is rent, and the great light of eternity begins to open to the soul wholly new horizons. Behold why death is the most beautiful moment in man's life. It is then he finds again all the virtues he has practised during life, all the strength and peace of which he has made provision, all the memories, all the cherished images, the sweetest regrets, and the most beautiful anticipations of God.

Yes, for the Irish, death is truly "*the most beautiful moment in life, when one finds again all the virtues he has practised.*"

To appreciate this, one should assist at the deathbed of an Irishman; hear his pious invocations, his acts of faith, hope, love, contrition, and perfect resignation to the holy will of God. To witness his energy in the midst of his sufferings, his peace and calm during the last ceremonies, one would say it was an exile preparing to return to his country. And then how eagerly he seizes the image of his crucified Saviour! how fervently he gazes upon it, pressing it to his lips and clasping it to his heart! How generously he offers to his God who died for him the sacrifice of his own life! Does not this act alone merit heaven?

It is truly among the Irish that we find that

"facility to die" which Tertullian remarks in the first Christians : "*Christiani mori expeditum genus.*" The author, sadly famous for his Life of Jesus, has said, with a respect which conceals remorse, with an envious yet hopeless admiration : "I would not have the life of a Christian, but I envy his death. At sight of this calm and glorious end, the soul is elevated and strengthened, we resume our esteem for human nature, we are convinced that it is a noble nature, and that there is reason to be proud of it." *

Such was the calm and glorious death of the pious Ozanam, who felt his end drawing near at Pisa. At the thought of all that he was about to leave, but also of all that he was about to find again in a better world, he made this prayer to God : "To-day I have attained my fortieth year, more than half an ordinary life. I know that I have a young and loving wife, a lovely child, excellent brothers, a second mother, many friends, an honorable career, labors just completed, to serve as a foundation for a work of which I have long dreamed. Which of these worldly affections must I immolate to Thee? Were I to sell my books to give their price to the poor, were I to conse-

---

* Renan, "Études Religieuses."

crate the remainder of my days to relieving the distressed, wouldst Thou be satisfied, Lord, and leave me the happiness of growing old with my wife and educating my child? . . . Ah! it is I whom Thou wishest. I come, Lord, I come!" *

"In 1830, during one of those terrible famines with which Ireland is visited from time to time, in a parish of one of the most remote counties an event took place which was truly sublime.

"The inhabitants of the parish had exhausted all their resources. Nothing remained. Absolutely starving, they awaited death as a happy release. Their worthy priest, after the example of the Good Pastor, refused to leave his flock; he remained with them, and implored with tears the assistance of heaven for his children. Finally a time came when nothing more could be expected from human sources. Then the priest, dragging himself from cabin to cabin, said:

"'My children, it is God who gives life, and it is God who takes it away. Come and die at His feet!'

"At these words fifteen hundred creatures, resembling spectres more than human beings, dragged themselves to the village church and,

---

* Letter of Ozanam, quoted by Lacordaire.

prostrated themselves before the tabernacle. The priest mounted the steps of the altar, and extending his emaciated hands over the heads of the dying, recited the litany for the agonizing and the prayers for the dead."

"Is there in all history anything comparable to the heroism of these poor villagers at the foot of the altar, finding in the simple blessing of the priest resignation and strength to die of hunger?" *

Besides these exceptional circumstances, one frequently witnesses at the deathbeds of the Irish the same *generosity* and the same *heroism*.

Hear the touching details of a death of this kind which took place at Nice a few years ago. It is related by the pen of an Irish lady:

"*December 25th.—Sic nos amantem quis non redamaret.*† Ellen ‡ went to heaven while René was singing these words after the midnight mass. This death is life and gladness. Lucy and I have prepared her for the tomb; we have clothed her in the white lace robe which was a present from her mother, and

---

* Montalembert, "Lettres sur le Catholicisme en Irelande."

† Who would not love him who has loved us so much?

‡ Ellen is the young married lady who has just died; Karl is her husband. René is the husband of the narrator. Lucy is a friend of the two families. Robert is the child of Karl and the deceased Ellen.

arranged for the last time her rich abundant hair. It is true, then, that all is over; those lips are closed forever. She died after receiving the Beloved of her soul. What a night it has been! I had a presentiment of this departure. For two days past I have lived in her room, scarcely taking my eyes off her face, and listening to her affectionate recommendations. On the 23d we spoke of St. Chantal—that soul so ardent, so eminently made for goodness, so heroic among all others, who had her full share of crosses, and who so truly knew how to love and suffer. On the 24th a swallow came and chirped on the marble of the chimney. 'I shall fly away like her, but I shall go to God,' Ellen murmured. At two o'clock that same day her confessor came, and we left her for a few moments. Toward three o'clock she seemed stronger; she took her husband's hand, and in a voice, the tender tones of which still resound in my ears, said to him, speaking very slowly : 'Remember that God remains to you, and that my soul will not leave you. Love God alone; serve Him in the way He wills. Robert and I will watch over your happiness.' She hesitated a moment; her whole soul was in her eyes. 'Tell me that *you will be a priest;* that instead of wrapping yourself in your sorrow you will spend yourself for the salvation of souls; you will spread the love of Him who gives me strength to leave you with joy to go to Him.' Karl was kneeling. 'I promise it before God,' he said. The color came to the pale face of the dying one, and she joined her hands in a transport of gratitude. She received all the dear neighbors and said a few heartfelt words to each. She asked the blessing of our dear mother, who would not be absent from us, and shared our joys and our sorrows. The doctor came. 'It will be to-morrow, if she can last until then,' he told René. O my God! And the night began — that solemn night of the angel's hosanna, of the birth of the Redeemer. I held one of her hands, Karl the other, my mother and René were near us, our brothers and sisters in the room which had been converted into a chapel. At eleven o'clock I raised the pillows and began to read, at Ellen's request, a sermon on death. After the first few lines she stopped me with a look; Karl had grown pale again. The dying loved one asked us to sing. We were so electrified by Ellen's calmness that we obeyed. She tried to join her voice with ours. The priest came; the mass began. Ellen, radiant, followed every word. We all received Holy Communion with her.

After the mass she embraced us all, keeping

Karl's head some time between her hands—her poor little alabaster hands; then, at her request, René sang the Adeste: *Sic nos amantem quis non redamaret?* As he uttered these words Ellen kissed the crucifix for the last time, and her soul took its flight to the bosom of God." *

Ah! when we witness a death like this we find that faith has the privilege to singularly transform even the saddest things in nature. We know not whether our tears are those of sorrow or joy; we know not whether to blame or bless our first parents for having introduced death by sin, and to praise God for permitting it. Did faith but serve to cause death to be accepted with resignation, or, what is more, with happiness and joy, yea with glad welcome and clapping of hands; † with hymns of praise

---

* "Letters of a Young Irishwoman to her Sister."

† There is no exaggeration in this. Toward the end of April, 1866, as I entered an educational institution at Lille, a young religious of the community, aged twenty-eight, was being carried to the cemetery. She had preserved her consciousness all during her agony. At the foot of her bed was her father and her young brother in tears. She made them a sign to approach, and in a faint voice, but with an angelic smile said, "Oh, dear father, dear little brother, why do you cry? Do as I do: thank God for my deliverance, clap your hands with joy for it; for this is the most beautiful day of my life; to-day I go to God." And the dying religious began to clap her hands.

on our own lips, and the lips of those about us. Yes, did Faith do but this it would be sufficient ; we should prostrate ourselves before God and cry : " My God, I thank Thee ! I thank Thee a thousand times for such a benefit."

CHAPTER IX.

DEATH OF HENRI DE KLEIST, A DISCIPLE OF KANT — DEATH OF THEOPHANE VENARD, APOSTOLIC MISSIONARY.

EHOLD Faith and her works! Let us compare such a death with the departure of those who are enemies to faith, or simply the victims of doubt. Some, like Rousseau and Condorcet, cowardly soldiers deserting their posts, put an end to their days; others, like Voltaire, breathed the last sigh in terrible convulsions of rage and despair. Let us recall particularly that disciple of Kant, Henri de Kleist, who in October, 1811, in the chamber of an inn on the lake of Vansee, near Potsdam, made the echoes ring with that double sound which sent him before the tribunal of God. Compare the language of this despairing soul with the sublime words of him who believes and hopes. His last night was spent writing to a few intimate friends; and on the brink of the eternal abyss he sneers at his soul, which he says, "like a happy aeronaut will rise above this world to fields resplendent

in light, where he will wander with wings at his shoulders." He writes also to his sister who, during long years had perseveringly shown him the tenderness and devotion of a mother. Here is all his heart prompts him to say in gratitude at such a moment : " to save me you have done not only all that a sister, but all that a man could do. The truth is, nothing on earth can help me. For the present, farewell !"

In 1861, on the eve of his martyrdom, a missionary writes also to his sister, who had loved him with an equal motherly devotion. What noble words are his ! Between the disciple of Kant and the disciple of Jesus Christ there is the distance of earth from heaven.

J. M. J. From my Cage at Tong-King.
January 20, 1861.

" My dear Sister : I wrote, a few days ago, a general letter to all the family, in which I gave several details of my capture and my examination ; this letter has already gone, and I hope reached you. Now that my end is approaching I wish to address a few lines of special farewell to you, dear sister and friend. For you know our hearts have been one from our childhood. You had no secrets from me, nor I from you, dear Melanie. When each year I left home for college, it was you who prepared my wardrobe and softened with tender words the pain of parting; it was you who shared my college joys and triumphs; it was you who seconded with fervent prayers my vocation as a missionary. It was with you, dear Melanie, that I spent the night of the 26th of February, our last interview upon earth, in sympathetic communings as sweet and as holy as those of St. Benedict and his saintly sister. And when I had crossed the seas to water with my sweat and my blood the Annamite soil, your letters, loving messengers, followed me regularly, to console me, to encourage me, to strengthen me. It is natural then that your brother, at this supreme moment which precedes his immolation, should remember you, dear sister, and desire to send you a special farewell. It is nearly midnight; about my cage are lances and long sabres. In a corner of the room is a group of soldiers playing cards, another group is playing with dice. From time to time a sentinel announces with the tam-tam and drum the watches of the night. A few feet from me a projecting lamp casts a flickering light on a sheet of Chinese paper, and enables me to trace these lines to you. I await my sentence from day to day. Perhaps to-morrow I will be led to execution. Is it not a happy death? Most enviable death which leads to life! In all probability I shall be beheaded—glorious ignominy of which the price is heaven. At this news you will weep, dear sister, but it must be with joy. Think of your brother with the aureole of the martyr on his brow, the palm of victory in his hand! A little while, and my soul will leave this earth, terminate her exile, finish her combat. I am going to heaven; I approach the celestial country; I bear off the victory; I am about to enter the abode of the elect, to gaze on beauty which the eye of man has never seen, to hear harmonies which ear has never heard, to experience joys which heart has never known. But the wheat must first be crushed in the mill-stone, the grape must be trodden in the wine-press. Shall I be wine and bread fit for the Master's use? I hope it, through the mercy of God and the protection of His Immaculate Mother; and it is this reliance which makes me, though still in the arena, venture to intone a hymn of triumph as though I were already a victor crowned.

"And you, dear sister, I leave you in the field of virtues and good works. Reap numerous merits for the same eternal life which awaits us both. Gather faith, hope, charity, patience, meekness, perseverance, and a holy death.

"Farewell, Melanie! Farewell, cherished sister. Farewell!

"Your brother,

"J. Th. Venard, *Miss. Apost.*" *

"Most admirable religion!" may we not exclaim with him who later was the poet of nothingness. "He is no true philosopher who does not respect and follow thee. I do not hesitate to say that he has no heart, that he feels not the sweet emotions of a perfect love, that he knows not the ecstasies of rapt meditation, who knows not how to love with transport, who does not feel himself drawn toward the ineffable Object of the worship thou teachest us. Thou wilt live forever, and error can never be with thee. When she shall assail us and seek to place her dark hand before our eyes; when she threatens to draw us into the yawning abyss opened at our feet by ignorance, we will turn to thee and we shall find light 'neath thy mantle. Error will fly to the mountain like a wolf pursued by the shepherd, and thy hand will lead us to salvation." †

* "Life and Correspondence of J. Theophane Venard."
† Léopardi, "Essai sur les Erreurs Populaires des Anciens."

CHAPTER X.

HOW DESERVEDLY IRELAND MERITS THE TITLE OF THE "VIRGIN ISLE"—HER CHARACTERISTIC VIRTUE.

F these marvels of the *generosity of the Irish* astonish us, let us remember that there is another virtue, daughter of faith, a virtue specially reserved to Catholics, a virtue wholly beautiful, wholly divine, which ineffably adorns the smile and glance of youth, which adds new majesty to the white hairs of the old man, which at every age places a crown of honor, an aureole of respect, on the brow of man. When it is a whole people who possess this noble privilege, we must expect to see in them, with strength, courage, generosity, and devotion, all the other virtues which make great nations.

Such is the glory of Ireland, and it is not the least. Near her is another isle, which formerly, in happier times, rejoiced in the name of the *Isle of Saints*, a glorious name which she has lost. She will merit it anew one day; everything leads us to hope it. In the eyes of God it will be of more value for her than if she were to establish her banks and her counting-houses in every region of the world.

As for Ireland, she merits to this day the beautiful name of the *Virgin Isle*.

We may apply to her the words in which the historian of St. Ambrose, Bishop of Milan, describes the brother of the bishop : " Simple as a child, pure as a virgin." *

" From the moment that this *Green Erin*, situated at the extremity of the known world, had seen the sun of faith rise for her, she vowed to it that ardent and tender devotion which became her very life. The course of ages has not interrupted it, the most bloody and implacable of persecutions has not shaken it, the defection of all northern Europe has not led her astray and she still maintains under the formidable power of Anglo-Saxon supremacy an inextinguishable centre of faith, where survives, together with the completest orthodoxy, *that admirable purity of morals* which no adversary has been able to dispute, to equal, or to diminish." †

There, in fact, that *admirable purity of morals* abides as in an impregnable fortress. Roman corruption has never dishonored it. When

---

* Abbé Bonard, "Vie de Saint Ambroise."
† Montalembert, "Monks of the West."

Christianity came to the land she had not, to oppose her, either dissolute morals or pagan vices. Ireland's was not a baptism of blood. "That *Virgin Isle* on which proconsul never set foot, which never knew either the orgies or exactions of Rome, was the only place in the world of which the Gospel took possession without, so to speak, resistance or bloodshed."*

Behold the spectacle which, as early as the twelfth century, forces from an enemy of Ireland, a British writer, this acknowledgment and beautiful tribute : " Among all the virtues which distinguish Ireland, that of *Chastity* holds the first rank." †

"Even to the present day one breathes an indescribable *perfume of virtue* among this people, which is not to be found elsewhere."‡

Strict morals, traditions of honor, respect for one's self, one's name, one's hearth, continue to be transmitted among the Irish from generation to generation as a sacred inheritance, as the holiest and most precious of all riches.

Consult the public records, seek the testimony of facts, question the people among, whom they live in America as elsewhere, it will be clearly manifest that weaknesses are almost

---

* Frederic Ozanam, " Études Germaniques."
† Giraldus Cambrensis.
‡ Mgr. Dupanloup.

unknown among them, that vice does not venture to appear. And when at rare intervals one of their number falls, and if there is no longer any doubt of the recent misfortune, the following Sunday, in the little village chapel or the city church a sad and at the same time beautiful scene takes place. At the end of one of the offices of the day, you will see the father and mother of the guilty one advancing in tears to the altar holding a lighted candle ; they devoutly kneel before the tabernacle, and publicly ask pardon of God and man for the scandal which their child has given.

Here is an incident which reveals the height to which *this generosity of the Irish faith* will rise at times. Its existence alone supposes an assemblage of virtues carried to heroism.

At the beginning of the winter of 1869, a young Irish girl took service in a house in New York. She had not been many hours among her new masters before she discovered from certain unmistakable evidences that it was anything but a respectable house. She seized the bundle which contained her wardrobe, and was about to rush from the house when the mistress met her, and not only refused to let her depart, but locked her in a third story room. The poor child, terrified at the danger which threatened her faith, and perhaps her innocence, fell on her knees, and after a short and fervent prayer opened the window and with her bundle on her arm sprang to the street. And God, who permitted not the flames to harm the children in the fiery furnace, nor the lions to approach Daniel ; who made wild beasts timid and playful as lambs at the feet of the martyrs— He who refuses nothing to one who gives all, sent His protecting angels * to sustain her in her fall. He saved the life of her who by an heroic act had saved her faith and her virtue.

O noble people, thou art truly worthy of that sublime hymn written in thy honor by the Louisiana bard,† that humble priest, learned missionary, and poet, who writes like Chateaubriand and sings like Lamartine.

> " Emerald of ocean and mystical jewel,
>   Glory and honor alone be thy due.
> Tho' heavy thy crosses and weary thy burden,
>   Thou ever remainest so great and so true.
> The land of the martyr, the land of O'Connell,
>   The saintliest spot 'neath the heaven's blue dome,
> O'er thee Faith's bright beacon is steadily glowing—
>   With thee, faithful Erin, Love has her home.
> Bearing on high the harp as thine emblem,
>   Thy heart ever answers to Liberty's plaint ;
> O Catholic Erin, O verdure-crowned island,
>   The blood of the Celt remains without taint.

---

* " For he hath given his angels charge over thee, to keep thee in all thy ways."—Ps. 90 : 12.

† Rev. A. Rouquette.

Thy children are exiles all the world over ;
  They carry the dear faith from sea unto sea.
O Chosen of Nations, amid all earth's people
  My muse offers greeting and honor to thee.
For Genius and Faith, sparkling gem of the ocean,
  Have sent gifts upon thee with bountiful hand ;
O fearless Hibernia, the home of the poet,
  Hail, Isle of the Saints, hail, ever-blessed land.
Near the soft-sighing breezes that ever blow o'er thee,
  Tara's harp will respond with its sweet melody ;
Though the tear-drops fall heavy beneath thy white garlands,
  Honored and glorious thou ever shalt be."

CHAPTER XI.

PATRIOTISM OF THE IRISH — IMPERISHABLE LOVE FOR THE MOTHER-COUNTRY.

A FEW words now on another quality which is one of the salient characteristics of the *Irish faith—Patriotism.*

Among all the sentiments which, deeply rooted in the human heart, make it great and noble, there is one which is more powerful, more invincible, more enduring than all the rest : this *is love of country*—love for that little corner of earth which was our cradle, which contains the bones of our ancestors, beside whom we hope to be laid ; it is the *urn of the heart*, as the poet says :

> " Quel ciel valut jamais le ciel qui nous vit naitre ?
>   Ce toil, ce nid chéri, ce paternel foyer,
> Qu'on aima tout petit, avant de rien connaitre,
>   Et que jamais, au loin, rien ne fait oublier ?" *

How dear the sunny skies that smiled upon our birth,
   How dear the happy home where first we saw the day !
O sheltered, cherished nest, O sweetest spot of earth,
   So loved before we knew, how dear when far away !

* Segur, " La Maison."

It is frequently stated in our day that religion destroys patriotism. Ignoble calumny! Religion, so far from narrowing the heart, dilates it; love for the terrestrial country increases or diminishes in the soul in proportion with her love for the heavenly country.

"Religion which blesses the first steps in life binds one to his native land with sweet and powerful ties. It is religion particularly which makes us love with a deep and tender love the memories of our childhood and family home, the cross on the tomb of the parent, the village church bell which we never hear in later years without being better for it. So far from weakening patriotism, it enlarges, purifies, and animates it." *

The same author develops and magnificently proves this thought. "Religion," he says, "makes it of precept to love all men; but she commands us first of all to love our neighbor; it is from this love that patriotism proceeds.

"History teaches that the most religious people were those who were most attached to the land of their fathers. Open the Bible; at every page the patriotism of the Jewish nation appears in the splendor of new fervor. At what period was love of country greater than

---

* J. D'Arsac; "Les Frères des Écoles Chrétiennes pendant la Guerre," 1870-71.

in the age of faith? Was it not faith which drove back from the frontiers of France the tide of Mussulman invasion, and brought back the flag of France from the centre of the enemy's power. Was it not faith which gave birth to Joan of Arc, and reconquered the soil of our country usurped by England? Who does not remember the invincible resistance which the patriotism of religious Spain offered to the conqueror of Austerlitz and Marengo? If the faith of France had been less cold the Teutonic invaders would have been resisted more earnestly, more tenaciously, and we would not have been compelled in 1871 to sign the saddest treaty in our history. And in that war was it not those who were most faithful to their religion who were the bravest defenders of the flag? Who, then, would venture to refuse a salute of honor to the heroic pontifical Zouaves?" *

The Irish furnish the best proof that *patriotism is* admirably *allied to faith:* that people who bear so deeply, I should say so passionately graven in their hearts the ineffaceable image and eternal memory of their country. Ah! one should see them when cruel necessity, the avarice of the landlords, sometimes famine,

* J. D'Arsac, Introduction of work quoted.

obliges them to expatriate themselves. Behold their tears, their sighs, their touching farewell when they look for the last time on their native land, from which they are obliged to tear themselves.

A poor old Irishman was cruelly turned out of his cabin; before crossing the beloved threshold he knelt and repeatedly kissed it; it seemed as though he could not tear himself from the asylum which had witnessed the sorrows as well as the joys of his life; his wife and children knelt at his side, and the same scene was repeated. The brutal executor of the law, impatient at these prolonged demonstrations, seized the old man by the arm and dragged him from the house. At this, parents and children controlling their tears, restraining the anguish of their sorrow-stricken souls, withdrew in silence to tread the path of exile. But from time to time their sobs burst forth afresh when they turned to look for the last time at their home, as if to bid it a last farewell, as if to say, "O sacred spot of earth! never will we forget thee! Never; it matters not whither fortune may drive us, never wilt thou be absent from our hearts."

No; the Irishman's country will never be absent from his heart. It will be present with him in the solitude in the depths of the American forests, amid the noisy bustle of the city; it matters not under what sun, to what land the tide of fortune may send him, the Irishman is always the same; he never has but one country—Ireland.

But this patriotism, so pure and ardent among them all, is perhaps more touching in the priest and woman. May it not be because in these two beings faith is best personified?

On holidays, whether religious or patriotic, when the young Irish girl puts on her best apparel, engraved on her rings or her bracelet is a touching device in the mother tongue of her native land: *Erin ma vournin, Erin go bragh!** Were you admitted to the intimacy of an Irish priest, and you were to glance at his table, you would frequently see there the broken harp of Ireland with this device: *It is voiceless!*

No, his country is never absent from the heart of an Irishman. She is ever present with him, whatever the distance between him and his native soil. When he bids farewell to his family, his home, his country, among the trunks of the future exile is one which he watches with jealous care: it is that which contains a few handfuls of earth from the native land he is leaving. Not infrequently they put

* Erin my darling, Erin for ever.

in some of the village turf, and when he has reached one of those distant forests of America where he seeks delivery from famine, where he looks forward to live and breathe his last sigh, he endeavors to make the green turf live again about his cabin that he may have the consolation of seeing once more, and showing to his children, turf from his beloved native land. Finally, when his last hour approaches he asks his family as a supreme consolation to lay him in the coffin on a bed of Irish soil. "We had earth from Ireland and moss from Gartan to adorn Ellen's coffin." *

And then, after generously contributing to Catholic works of every kind, as we have shown, do you know how the Irish devote the remainder of their resources? Every year, and frequently even every month, he sends the result of his labor to an old dying father in Ireland, to a poor mother, to brothers and sisters whom he left there in misery, and for whose sake he has not feared to brave the bitterness of exile.

How far is this pious generosity carried? In truth, I would not venture to say, for fear of being charged with exaggeration, if it had not been publicly stated in an official report read in the English Parliament.†

---

* "Letters of a Young Irishwoman to her Sister."
† Parliamentary report quoted in "Transactions of the

Their patriotic love for the mother-country is expressed each year by a cipher more eloquent than words—five millions of dollars.

"In a quarter of a century (from 1843 to 1868) the Irish settled in America have managed to send to relatives living in Ireland a sum of money no less than twenty-four million pounds sterling, thus giving proof of an admirable spirit of economy, charity, and love of family inspired by religion, to which they cling with their whole heart."*

The Irish of New York have decided that this year,† owing to the famine which desolates their mother-country, they will not celebrate St. Patrick's Day, though it is a privation to their faith and their patriotism. The funds usually devoted to this purpose will be sent to Ireland. The greater number of the Irish societies in the different cities of the United States have imitated this noble example.

Is there generosity anywhere to be compared to it? Let them come now and tell us that Catholicism destroys patriotism! O Irish poet, illustrious Moore! thou hast reason to sing of

---

Relief Committee of the Society of Friends during the Famine in Ireland." Dublin, 1852.

* Maguire, quoted in the "Annals of the Religious World," October, 1879.

† 1880.

thy unhappy country ; to exclaim, doubtless in tears, but with a heart filled with national pride, love, and hope :

"Remember thee ! Yes, while there's life in this heart
It shall never forget thee, all lorn as thou art ;
More dear in thy sorrow, thy gloom and thy showers,
Than the rest of the world in their sunniest hours.

"Wert thou all that I wish thee—great, glorious, and free—
First flower of the earth and first gem of the sea—
I might hail thee with prouder, with happier brow,
But, oh ! could I love thee more deeply than now ?

"No, thy chains as they rankle, thy blood as it runs
But make thee more painfully dear to thy sons—
Whose hearts, like the young of the desert bird's nest,
Drink love in each life-drop that flows from thy breast !"

CHAPTER XII.

THE CONFRATERNITY OF THE IMMACULATE HEART OF MARY IN NEW YORK—ITS ESTABLISHMENT IN CHICAGO.

HO can tell the *power* of that magnanimous faith which stops at no sacrifice? It seems impossible for the heart of God to refuse it anything.

At the French church in New York there has been canonically established the *Irish Association* of the Holy Heart of Mary for the conversion of sinners, affiliated with the archconfraternity of Our Lady of Victories in Paris. Its members meet the first Sunday of every month at eight o'clock in the evening. It is needless to say that the church is crowded; but what I wish to add is that miracles of grace are ordinary occurrences in the society. I am embarrassed to make a choice from the numerous instances before me.

During the winter of 1870 a priest in New York had visited as many as fifteen times an unfortunate Frenchman, the father of a family, and dangerously ill. His efforts to bring him back to God had been fruitless. All the family, moreover, had been educated with infidel ideas. The boy, a child of twelve, asked the priest with a mocking smile and the air of a young Voltaire, "Can you remit sins? you?" not knowing that Jesus Christ Himself had long ago answered this same question, which was put to Him by the Jews. The daughter, a girl of fifteen, made threats, and confided to a neighbor her sinister projects of vengeance if the priest did not soon cease his frequent visits. The worthy mother of such children asked in her turn if one could not be absolved without confession. As for the sick man himself, his invariable answer to all the priest's charitable exhortations was, "I do not believe that."

After so many fruitless efforts, when the day for the meeting of the archconfraternity arrived there was most earnestly recommended to the prayers of the members a *hardened sinner* who was dying without the sacraments. Three days after, the dying man himself sent for the priest, made his confession, received Communion and the last sacraments with edifying piety. During all the ceremony he repeatedly kissed the crucifix and pressed it to his bosom. The earnestness of his gratitude and the extraordinary fervor of his repentance drew tears from the eyes of those who witnessed his last moments, even from those who at first appeared so little susceptible of emotion.

About the same time an Irishwoman came to the director of the Archconfraternity and said to him : " Father, for thirty years my husband has been the victim of a passion which impoverishes and ruins us." In fact her husband's passion for drink had swallowed up all the resources of the family. The poor mother alone supported the family by labor above her strength. Two weeks after, the erring father presented himself at the tribunal of penance and became a changed man. From that time the family have regained happiness, peace, and prosperity.

Another day a little girl nine years of age greeted the director of the Archconfraternity and said : " Father, I beg of you to ask the prayers of the association to-morrow evening for my mother ; she has gone away from home and left her seven little children, on account of my father's bad conduct. Oh ! tell them to ask the Blessed Virgin to bring us back our mother !" Sunday evening the unfaithful mother was made the object of the desired recommendation. It was not long before the prayers of the Irish were answered ; hardly a few days had passed before the despairing woman returned to her post. The little girl did not forget her duty of gratitude. She went in all haste to the confidant of her trouble, and finding him in the confessional cried, through the grating, in tones of inexpressible happiness : *Thank you, father, my mother came back.*

One day after Vespers in New York, I received a visit from two French ladies. In the course of conversation one of them, who was quite pious, said to me : " I am sure you have no idea that my sister here has not been to the sacraments for eight years." I made an evasive reply. That day the Archconfraternity was to meet. As soon as the ladies were gone, I went at once to the director and made him promise to recommend in a special manner to the prayers of the Irish, a *French lady estranged* from the sacraments. In the course of the week the subject of their prayers came to ask me my day and hour for hearing confessions.

In a voyage to France I related a series of similar facts to the director of the Archconfraternity of Our Lady of Victories at Paris. He replied, in a tone of conviction which impressed me very much : " I am not at all surprised at what you tell me. Establish the Archconfraternity everywhere in your missions, and everywhere you will see the same results, if you keep as the object of your prayers the first and necessary end of the association—the conversion of sinners!"

I beheld the words of the venerable priest verified in a most remarkable manner.

In the May of 1870 I gave a mission at Chicago.* At this mission, which was specially recommended to the prayers of the Irish Archconfraternity of New York, in addition to the evening sermon there was a short address each morning to the pious souls who assisted at mass. Every day I insisted on the necessity of canonically establishing in the parish, as a souvenir of the mission, the Archconfraternity of the Holy Heart of Mary, affiliated to the Confraternity of Our Lady of Victories in Paris. I repeatedly said to them: "Evil has become all-powerful in our day, because of its societies and organizations. Let the children of light here imitate the children of darkness. Let us unite to combat them; availing ourselves of the all-powerful weapon of an organization of prayer, we will be strong and victorious."

* This city, which forty years ago was a little village of twenty frame cabins inhabited by a few Indian fishermen, contains to-day a population of 600,000 souls. From its geographical position on Lake Michigan, about 1048 miles from New York, it is destined to become the metropolis as well as the natural centre of the commerce of the Western States.

After three successive appeals the faithful parishioners came in hundreds to have their names inscribed in the association.

One morning, just before my sermon, a young girl came to me in tears. "Father," she said, "my brother is dying; the doctor says he has not a week to live. He has not practised his religion for twenty years; and now he is not only indifferent, but he feels a hatred in his heart for religion. The day before yesterday he peremptorily ordered from his sight a good priest whom we brought to see him. To-day he still refuses to let any one speak to him of the sacraments. Father, you said that the Blessed Virgin would refuse no conversion to the Archconfraternity; then ask them to earnestly pray for my poor brother's conversion." I at once made known to the assistants the keen sorrow of this new Martha pleading for the resurrection of another Lazarus. "They want us to ask the first grace through the intercession of the Blessed Virgin, and we are not yet canonically established; but no matter, we will unite our prayers for the spiritual resurrection of this young man. I cannot doubt for a moment that the Blessed Virgin will hear us; she will prove to us that she desires the establishment of the Archconfraternity here. Let us kneel down and recite together for the dying man three Hail Marys and the aspiration, 'Oh! Mary, conceived without sin, pray for us who have recourse to thee,' three times."

It was then ten o'clock in the morning. An hour after, the sister of the dying man came to the rectory to say that her brother earnestly asked for a priest.

The pastor hastened to him, and as he approached the bedside the young man extended his hand, and with tears in his eyes at once made a confession of all his sins, with truly edifying contrition. On leaving him the priest said: "I will return in a few moments and bring you Holy Communion." "Father," he replied, "please leave me two hours to prepare to receive Almighty God."

During these two hours the mother and sister, at the sick man's request, read the prayers before Holy Communion. He had all profane pictures removed from his room that he might have before his eyes only the image of the Blessed Virgin. When he had received the last sacraments, the priest said to him, "Are you contented?" "Ah! father, more than contented," he replied. "I am happy! I had never loved God. To-day I love Him with my whole soul: that is the reason of my happiness."

CHAPTER XIII.

WHENCE THE IRISH REAP THE NUMEROUS AND EMINENT QUALITIES OF THEIR FAITH — THEIR VIGILANT OBSERVANCE OF RELIGIOUS PRACTICES — THE HEROIC CONSTANCY WHICH IRELAND HAS DISPLAYED IN THE DEFENCE OF HER FAITH UNRIVALLED IN THE ANNALS OF MANKIND—ASSOCIATION FOR THE CATHOLIC COLONIZATION OF THE IRISH IN AMERICA.

FROM *what sources*, then, do the Irish gather the *numerous and eminent qualities of their faith?*

No doubt they partly owe the precious treasure of that lively and ardent faith to the holy bishops who planted the Gospel among them. Do not the names alone of St. Patrick and St. Malachy recall a whole life of supernatural marvels? A book would hardly contain their number. St. Malachy called one day to see a sick man, hears his confession, but retires without giving him the last sacraments. A few hours afterward they come to tell him that the sick man has breathed his last. The holy bishop in much grief retraces his steps, and falling on his knees beside the coffin, addresses a fervent prayer to heaven, shedding abundant tears, then rising he commands death to give up its victim. The dead man opens his eyes, returns to life, receives Extreme Unction, then returns once more to his last sleep.

Behold the saints who have made the Irish people! Behold the masters in whose schools they were trained to the fulfilment of their religious duties!

But the cause of their perseverance in the faith, the reason of the transmission of this inestimable treasure in all its integrity from generation to generation, is their vigilant observance of *religious practices*. They are in fact the food and support of true faith. No doubt each taken separately is not strictly necessary, but taken jointly they strengthen and perpetuate faith. Thus each separate root of a great tree is not necessary to its life, but all these roots together give to the tree the sap and power of vegetation. When the storm comes the tree stands firm, strongly anchored by its numerous subterranean roots. It is the same with Christian faith, it possesses roots which when storms sweep over it serve as anchors to keep it fast and preserve it from shipwreck. Those who understand nothing of spiritual things have only a disdainful smile, a mocking sneer for those *humble practices of faith.*

To be logical they should hold in equal contempt the elementary exercises of the young recruit. This young soldier, who executes the first exercises in the profession of arms, the movements of the head, chest, hands, and feet, with so much awkwardness, may one day be a great hero, a marshal of France; but he must be exercised in these rudimentary practices.

Now the exercises and military manœuvres of the young soldier are like the daily practices of the Christian. If the soldier be not well exercised in the details of the use of his arms, how can he meet the enemy on the day of battle? Defeat is certain, for he is raw and unpractised. In like manner to triumph over temptation and preserve his faith intact, the Christian must be well exercised in religious practices. If we have no contempt for military exercises, we have no more reason to blame, criticise, or despise the exercises of a Christian. If the first make heroes, the latter make saints. And then every day of our lives are we not influenced by this doctrine? Do we not attach much the greatest value to details?

Here are two beautiful roses. Why do we give the preference to this one rather than that? Have they not the same form, the same stem, the same colors? Doubtless, but in one there is a delicate shade which charms the eye ; there is an arrangement, a disposition, a mingling of the colors which makes the whole more agreeable. It is a little detail, but it suffices to captivate us, and is precisely what communicates to the flower all its charm.

God acts in the same way toward us. He ceases not to look down lovingly from heaven upon each of His children, but he also has His predilections. According as we are more or less perfect, more or less accomplished in the details of our lives, we are more or less dear to Him. Like ourselves He deigns to be captivated by the perfect finish of the details.

Behold one of the causes of the preservation of the faith among the Irish. They are most faithful to the humblest practices of Christianity ; therefore it is that God has blessed them by granting them the greatest of all blessings—perseverance in faith.

It is not a rare thing in our day to hear men of mature age complain, *I have no faith.* Some add, *I would like to believe.*

I have no faith. Yet most frequently the man who speaks thus has possessed faith. As a child he believed in the religion of his mother; at her knee he joined his hands in prayer to the *God who rejoiced his youth.* Did he not believe on the thrice happy day of his first Communion? Long afterward he continued to be the joy of his mother, the edification of the parish. How he then loved his religion, its minister, his faith; how beautiful he found it: that faith which inspired the greatest poets, which animated the Crusades, which has made fruitful every great work! The youth already nourished in his soul great dreams for the future: "When I am a man what shall I do?" he would ask himself. "Ah! I will gird on a sword and go forth to make my body and my blood a rampart against the invasion of evil. Soldier of France, defender of the eldest daughter of the Church, I will further the *Gesta Dei per Francos.**

"When I am a man, what shall I do? I will take the chisel of the sculptor; I will give life to stone and marble; I will cause them to repeat the accents of the faith of saints; I will take the brush of the painter, and in the colors of the canvas I will repeat to my brothers in Jesus Christ the fervor of St. Jerome, the repentant tears of Magdalen, the raptures, the ecstasies of a Theresa, of a Francis of Assisi.

"When I am a man, what shall I do? Ah! if God in His infinite mercy will deign to purify

---

* The acts of God through the French.

my lips with a burning coal as he did the lips of the prophets, I also will ascend the altar and immolate the *Divine Victim* for the salvation of the world. I will be a priest ! And then, cost what it may, I will tear myself from the tenderness of my mother, from the love of home ; I will cross the seas ; I will scale the mountains ; I will go to the ends of the earth to repeat the wonders of my faith, to convert the savages in the depths of distant forests. Yes, I will be an apostle ; perhaps a martyr."

Alas ! how these dreams have vanished !

In place of this holy religious enthusiasm, only culpable indifference remains. What has effected this ruin ? Whence is this cry to-day : *I have no faith!*

The child grew. Soon he was seen to take his place in assemblies where altars are raised to vice. There he encountered those who calumniated the faith of his fathers, who insulted religion and its ministers. He frequented theatres where religion and morality were held up to derision. He returns to the parental roof, where he encounters the enemy of his faith in all things : the enemy in the library, where, side by side with the Bible, the prayer-book, the Following of Christ, are the complete works of Voltaire ; the enemy on the walls, whence the image of Christ has been removed—

an adornment doubtless too ancient, too austere for a century of progress—and replaced by pictures from which a true Christian must turn his eyes; the enemy, finally, on the table of the *salon*, where he finds only bold calumniating journals, impure literature, books of subtle poison, scandalous romances fitted to enkindle the fire of passion in the purest hearts. How can faith survive under the daily infusion of these accumulated poisons? How can the mind fail to be darkened, the will weakened, the heart degraded, and virtue destroyed?

Place a thick veil before your eyes, and all will be darkness about you. If you accumulate mountains of error before the eyes of your soul, you blind them; how, then, can you expect that they will see the pure rays of truth? When you stir the waters of a stagnant pool, it sends forth pestilential vapors and miasma, which corrupt the air and sow disease and death in their passage. In like manner, when the evil passions are overexcited the heart languishes and is corrupted under the influence of sensual impressions. Then man, becoming wholly carnal, in the energetic words of St. Paul, understands not the things of God. He *has no faith*, but you must acknowledge that he has done everything to destroy it and nothing to preserve it.

And now of those who add, *I would like to believe*, may we not ask what do you do to acquire faith? What good works do you perform? What religious practices do you impose upon yourself each day? What sacrifices do you make? You desire the end, but you will not take the means. Your desire will never be realized ; here again you will be the author of your own unhappiness.

Oh ! how different is the conduct of the Irish people ! What sacrifices of every description have they not made, and do they not make every day to preserve intact this precious treasure of faith which they justly prize above all things?

" The heroic constancy which Ireland has displayed in the defence of her faith is unrivalled in the annals of mankind. No race under the sun has struggled longer or more obstinately against religious persecution." *

" One of the misfortunes of the human race which excites most sympathy is the loss of nationality. There is something so sacred in the thought of country that when we read in history of one of those periods when God by an inscrutable judgment withdraws the life of a nation, we are seized with such a compassionate

---

* Montalembert's " Monks of the West."

love for the failing country disappeared long ages since, that we long for her resuscitation as if it were our own. We would aid its unhappy defenders; we envy the fate which laid them in the earth, and that melancholy glory with which a vanquished people enshrouds the tombs of her last heroes. . . . It is indeed a spectacle for tears, the end of a great nation. Conquerors themselves are not insensible to it. Scipio wept at the fall of burning Carthage, and when astonishment was expressed at his sorrow, replied, 'I am thinking of the time when this day shall come for Rome!' Religion, accustomed as it is to witness the end of nations and men, has secret and tender tears for these great misfortunes which attest the decay of all." *

"This great misfortune," loss of country, Ireland has endured to preserve her faith. The *virgin*, the *apostle nation*, has also become a *martyr nation*. Crowned with this triple diadem, more beautiful than that of kings, she has risen to a sublime height of greatness.

"Men and families have been seen to die for their faith, and from this grand spectacle leave behind them only their mutilated remains and stainless memory. But an entire nation living

---

* Lacordaire, "Lettre sur la Sainte Siege."

in continual martyrdom, generations of souls bound together by national ties, transmitting the inheritance of faith through an inheritance of suffering, is a spectacle which had not been witnessed. God has willed it, and effected it. He willed it in our day, and it has been effected in our day. Among the nations threatened with spiritual bondage, there is one which has not accepted the yoke, which, enslaved in body, has remained free in soul. One of the proudest powers of the world has struggled hand to hand with her, to drag her into the abyss of schism and apostasy. Doomed to a war of extermination, she has yielded to it without ever failing in the courage of battle or courageous fidelity to God. Despoiled of her native land by gigantic confiscations, she has cultivated for her conquerors the fields of her ancestors, and in the sweat of her brow gained the bread which sufficed her to live in honor and die in faith. Famine disputed this crust with her; she lifted toward Providence eyes which reproached Him not. Neither war, spoliation, nor famine has caused her to perish or apostatize; her oppressors, powerful as they were, have not been able to crush her vital life, or drive duty from her heart." *

* Lacordaire's Panegyric of O'Connell.

What is the eloquent cipher which expresses the sacrifices of this martyr people?

On the 25th of July, 1861, the highest officer of the crown in Ireland, the Lord Lieutenant, acknowledged in an official address that in twenty years, from 1841 to 1861, by ejections as well as emigration 366,000 country dwellings had disappeared.*

During the same lapse of time the Irish population has diminished two and a half millions. Five hundred thousand, at least, have died of hunger; the others have gone to people North America and Australia. To-day the Irish, while enjoying far from their homes the liberty which cost them so dear, do not cease to watch over the preservation of their faith.

In the last few years a great movement has taken place among the Irish people in America. They are leaving the populous cities and flocking to the fertile countries of the West. This is the result of an admirable society known as the "Association for the Catholic Colonization of the Irish in America."

It is only the work of yesterday. It first originated with an American prelate, Bishop Ireland, the coadjutor of the diocese of St. Paul. The marvellous results obtained in a

---

* An address delivered at Cork by the Lord Lieutenant of Ireland.

short time on a small scale led to a great enterprise. A gigantic mass meeting was held at Chicago in which the "Association for the Colonization of Irish Catholics in America" was legally organized. Bishop Spalding of Peoria was made president; it was decided that the association would take no steps until they had raised $100,000. This sum was soon realized. At another meeting held in New York a remarkable report was presented by the president of the work. Forty American prelates, bishops, and archbishops had assembled in New York for the consecration of the new cathedral. They all assisted at the meeting, and promptly gave their approbation and encouragement to the work.

"The Irish," said the report, "are essentially an agricultural people. Yet until to-day the fertile lands of the West have been invaded, taken possession of, by other people, while the Irish have continued to vegetate in the great cities, where they die for want of air and work. Let them in their turn seek these Western regions. They will find a purer air, a more social, less corrupt atmosphere, and above all a soil which will yield a hundredfold to their labor."

But an advance in money is required to enable the emigrant to reach the West, and also to meet his first expenses, for it requires at least a year of hard labor before he can support himself. The Irish Catholic Association solves this difficulty. It takes upon itself all the expenses of the transportation and complete settlement of the emigrant. Each one is assigned forty acres of productive land, in the centre of which is a house with all its appurtenances. He takes possession of his farm at sowing time, and in four months he is able to exchange his first harvest for ready money. Little by little the colonist returns what was advanced to him, and becomes a land-owner. Does not such an organization merit the sympathy of all?

But the *end of the society is more admirable still.* What is this end? Is it solely to contribute to the temporal welfare and comfort of the Irish? The organization was formed for a higher and nobler end.

Let us resume in a few words the considerations laid before the meeting in Chicago on the day when the association was organized. The main object of the organization is the preservation of Catholic faith and morality in all its purity. In this respect the association is an *urgent necessity.*

Behold the end concisely stated. The prospectus of the association states it no less clearly. " The advantages of the society have long been appreciated by the wisest and best friends of the emigrants. The Irishman on landing in America, if he meets no one to persuade him otherwise, naturally settles in the large cities, the centres of all vice. At any price he must be taken thence, and wrested from occasions which peril his faith and his virtue."

The veritable object of this association, then, is to *save the faith* of the Irish emigrant in America.

Is it astonishing, then, that a people preserve the pious traditions of their fathers, who so thoroughly comprehend the fundamental law of progress laid down by Christ Himself : *Seek first the kingdom of God ?*

What is this *kingdom ?* Is it not the reign of truth enlightening the mind with supernatural light ; the reign of the decalogue placing a salutary restraint on human passion and the caprices of the *will;* the reign, finally, of charity, that heavenly virtue, the mother of all devotion and the source of the most generous inspirations of the *heart.* The logical, not to say the material result of following this law is, as the Master affirms, the possession of all things indispensable to human life : clothes, food, and all these things. *Seek first the kingdom of God, and all these things shall be added unto you.*

CHAPTER XIV.

HOW THE FAITH OF THE IRISH ENABLES THEM TO TRIUMPH OVER THEIR NATIONAL FAILING.

ALAS! why, even in the midst of its grandest qualities, must our poor humanity always manifest some remains of original weakness?

I have celebrated the virtues of the Irish, and those who know them will not accuse me of exaggeration. Truth now compels me to acknowledge that there is a shadow in the picture. Perfection is not of earth; it is only to be found in heaven.

A weakness too well known shadows the pure horizon of the Irish faith. But I hasten to add, with the author of an excellent work : *

"If a certain number of the Irish are subject to this weakness, it must be acknowledged that they generously redeem it by noble virtues." There is no people so glorious that must not at times draw the sword from the scabbard to

---

* "Sick Calls," Dr. Price.

keep in subjection the nations they have conquered. There is no man so perfect but he must needs draw the spiritual sword to keep in subjection the enemy which each one bears within himself. Did not God leave tribes of the enemy about Israel to maintain the zeal and courage of His people? Did not the Romans refuse to destroy Carthage, their rival, that they might not fall into effeminacy, but remain a warlike people through the necessity of being ever ready for battle? The Irish also have their *Carthage!*

"That they have this fault I acknowledge; but in the words of a contemporary publicist published in a celebrated review,* the Irish at least are not base, they are still noble, and nobility with sanctity is the most beautiful flower of the soul." † This nobility consists in recognizing their miseries, confessing them, repenting of them, correcting them, making them serve as means to advance a degree higher on the ladder of perfection.

Faith enables the Irishman to gain the greatest of victories—victory over himself, over a fault which too often in many turns to a passion, blinds them and drives them into the path of ruin and dishonor.

* Dr. Newman, *Catholic University Gazette.*
† Mgr. Dupanloup.

In America what priest has not had an Irishman come to him in shame and confusion to confess his weakness. But the humiliating avowal of his unfortunate habit is accompanied with a request that the *pledge* may be administered to him. He solemnly promises the minister of God to renounce for the future all use of intoxicating liquors. The priest then takes him to the church, and after a few words of exhortation, in which he reminds him of the dangers to which his unhappy passion exposes him, and suggests the means of perseverance, the culprit kneels and the pledge is administered to him for a certain fixed time. It must be added that the solemn promise thus made is generally kept with scrupulous fidelity.

Sometimes, instead of this private pledge, the Irishman, to gain new courage against himself, makes a solemn, so to speak, public promise by enrolling himself in a society which is unknown in France, the *Total Abstinence Society*. Whoever inscribes his name in this association is obliged to refrain from the use of beer, ale, wine, and all intoxicating liquors. In a large number of parishes these societies are very flourishing. On days of public rejoicing they figure with flying banners, on which is represented a portrait of Father Mathew, the great preacher and apostle of *total abstinence*.

In 1870 one of my fellow-laborers in New York was returning from bringing holy Communion to a sick man, when he was stopped at a turn in the stairway by a woman who, pointing to a neighboring apartment, begged him to enter for a moment. It was nine o'clock in the morning ; a man was getting up, and five little children were going to and fro in the same room. The woman was the first to speak, and said to the priest, pointing with a vehement gesture to her husband, " Father, look at that wretched man ! He is a bad husband, a bad father, for he drinks and does nothing for the support of his family. I can no longer support and educate by myself five little children. Oh ! father, speak to him, make him understand that he must give up the life he is leading."

At these last words the husband exclaimed : " Father, look at that woman ; she is the real culprit ! She drinks harder than I do ; it is she who has been my ruin ; it was through her that I contracted the habit of drinking ; I never drank before I was married. Father, if you could convert her it would be a good work. Speak to her. I say, as she does, that there must be an end to this kind of life."

" You are both right, and you are both wrong," said the priest. " I call upon God to witness your happy dispositions. If I have understood you, you ask for the pledge. Kneel down, both of you, and say with me, 'I renounce before God my guilty habit.'"

The couple knelt and made the solemn promise. A few weeks after the same priest went to visit the family. Imagine his surprise to see them all seated round a table, content and happiness visible in every countenance.

"Ah! I came to see how you were getting on," said the priest; "but let me congratulate you at once. The pleasant picture I see before me tells its own story."

"Father," replied the husband, "I thank you in the name of myself and my family. From the day we took the pledge everything has gone well with us. I am working and saving. I have money, but, above all, I have a peaceful home."

Behold the courageous faith of the Irish, which enables them to gain such victories over themselves!

How many times we hear men who are strangers to religious sentiments utter these sad words: *What use is religion?*

Would they but give themselves the trouble to reflect, how easily they could find a reply to this question: *What use is religion?* It serves to wrest man from his evil habits and degradation; it restores him to true liberty by breaking the chains of vice, and giving him the sweet joys of virtue ; it restores to children the right to their parents' love, instruction, and care ; it restores peace, and gives new life to families. Are not such results sufficient to forever silence her calumniators?

What religion effects in individuals and families it would equally effect in society, would society but follow her wise and salutary maxims.

CHAPTER XV.

THE SYMPATHY AND UNION WHICH HAVE ALWAYS EXISTED BETWEEN THE IRISH AND THE FRENCH—EXTRACT FROM "THE LETTERS OF A YOUNG IRISHWOMAN TO HER SISTER"—THE WIT OF THE IRISH IN REPARTEE—LETTER OF THE NUN OF KENMARE.

ND now if a word be needed to complete the glory of this *Irish faith*, I would willingly add: this *faith is French!*

It has been said: "Every man has two countries, his own and then France!"* These words are particularly true in the case of the Irish. We had ample proof of it in America during our last reverses. We were in adversity, and found ourselves alone. The false friends of yesterday deserted us, or at least feared to longer acknowledge us; the words of the poet were again verified:

* Henri Bornier, "La Fille de Roland."

"Donec eris felix multos numerabis amicos ;
Tempora si fuerint nubila . . . solus eris !" *

Doubtless they had suddenly passed from admiration of us to jealousy, then to pity bordering on contempt at the news of our humiliations. One people alone had ever the courage to manifest their sympathy with us ; they visibly suffered like us and with us. This was the *Irish people*. From the highest to the humblest among them their word for us was always : *Poor France ! God save France !* In a collection made at the French church in New York in behalf of our wounded, poor Irish laborers were seen to give as much as $5. And during the National French Bazaar, held at New York after the war, and of which the first evening's receipts were $22,000, the Irish spent their money with princely generosity.

The sentiments of the hearts of the entire nation were expressed by an Irish pen : " Italy, France, Ireland, the three countries of my soul —lands that mingle as one in my enthusiasm and love, daughters of God, favorites of my heart—you cannot perish ; God will fight for you, and we shall bless Him forever."

Moreover, the Irish do not forget, for they

---

* Ovid. "In prosperity your friends will be numerous, in adversity you will be alone."

have the memory of the heart. What they did was done in gratitude. Where was there greater sympathy than in France during the last three centuries for the evils of every description which the martyr nation endured?

A few years ago Mgr. Mermillod was eloquently pleading before a large and sympathetic audience the noble cause of the poor of Ireland. It was a time when they were again enduring the cruel sufferings of hunger. On hearing the moving recital of the woes of the suffering country generous souls were touched, and when the earnest appeal was ended all made generous offerings of alms. A poor workman also desired to share in this demonstration " of charity and gratitude." He followed the elegant assembly, and approaching one of the brilliant ladies who collected the alms, handed her his watch, with these heroic words : " What need have I to know the hour, when a people are dying of hunger !"

It is not astonishing, moreover, that the French and Irish should be a nation of brothers ; the parentage is evident not only because there is found in them some of the old Gallic blood, and valiant character of our ancestors, but particularly because Ireland and France divide the apostleship of the world. " By their common devotedness these two daughters of the Catholic Church are recognized as sisters."*

These two sister nations began by reciprocally exchanging the great blessing of faith, which they were to propagate later in every part of the globe : " We sent them St. Patrick, who converted their ancestors with thirty Breton missionaries recruited by him in the great neighboring isle, and they became his coadjutors or successors in the episcopacy. After thirty-three years of apostleship he died,† leaving Ireland almost entirely converted, and filled moreover with schools and communities destined to become a nursery of missionaries for the West." ‡

Thus toward the end of the sixth century the spiritual action of Ireland became decisive upon all the countries directly subjected to Frank dominion. It was then that she generously repaid her ancient debt to Gaul. We had given her St. Patrick ; she sent us in return St. Columbanus. That illustrious monk, the inheritor of the Irish apostle's zeal, founded the celebrated monastery of Luxeuil, which sent forth innumerable colonies of religious, who cleared our forests and planted the faith among our ancestors.

---

* Mgr. Dupanloup. † March 17, 465.
‡ Montalembert's " Monks of the West."

This ancient spiritual parentage explains why the French priest loves to work side by side with the Irish priest. The latter in his turn always finds a second country in France. It was an Irishman, the Abbé Edgeworth, who robbed us French priests of the sad but enviable honor of accompanying the royal martyr at the last supreme moment, of mounting the scaffold with him and addressing him those immortal words : " Son of St. Louis, ascend to heaven !" Several French ecclesiastics, it is true, coveted this honor. The Abbé Legris-Duval, of venerated and sweet memory, presented himself to the revolutionary committee with the hope of being admitted to the king. He even waited all night at the entrance to the committee, bearing over his heart in a sacred vessel the Holy Eucharist ; but he was unsuccessful : the Irish priest had forestalled him.

Admirable emulation ! heavenly rivalry ! that of two priests contesting in the face of the scaffold, so to speak, the honor of assisting in the salvation of a soul. It is the living and veritable image of these two nations, apostles, and missionaries both of them ; " those two daughters of the Catholic Church, who by their common devotion are recognized as sisters," and share the noble mission of carrying the Gospel throughout the world.

Thus, because of this old and powerful sympathy, of this common vocation of apostleship, of this reciprocal exchange of the blessings of faith, how frequently have the Irish fought under our flag! Upon how many battle-fields has the blood of Ireland mingled with that of France!

In our long wars under Louis XIV., the Duke de St. Simon says "the Irish battalion did wonders."

"From a report made to the minister of war," says an Irish historian who wrote in 1763, "we find that from the introduction of Irish troops into France in 1691 until 1745, the year of the battle of Fontenoy, more than 450,000 Irishmen have died in the service of France."

Behold why Louis XIV., in an outburst of royal and just gratitude, desired to naturalize in a measure the whole army of James II.

"We will," he writes, "that Irishmen should enjoy the same privileges as Frenchmen, without requiring naturalization papers."

Who is ignorant of the eminent service they rendered us at the famous battle of Fontenoy; how far they contributed to the victory of that great day, and how they wrung from the vanquished King of England, George II., that cry of a tardy and fruitless repentance: "Cursed be the laws which deprives me of such soldiers!"

But if these laws were cursed by the King of England, they were not by the King of France. It is said, however, that there were many turbulent spirits and hot heads among them who were not always easy to manage, so that they might be compared to our modern Zouaves. One day M. d'Argenson went to complain of them to the king. "Sire," he said, "that one Irish brigade gives me more to do than all the rest of the army." "But that is exactly what all my enemies say of them," immediately answered Louis XV.

In the course of this work I have quoted several passages from a volume entitled "Letters of a Young Irishwoman to her Sister."

This young girl was born in Ireland. She never knew her father, and her mother died when she was young. The affection of an elder sister replaced that of the family she lost, until a happy and brilliant marriage fixed her destiny in France. A few days after, the generous sister, obedient to a vocation which called her to the service of God, entered a religious house, and then began between the two sisters a correspondence which even death did not end. It is from this correspondence that I have several times quoted.

The brilliant marriage of the young Irish girl took place in 1867. He with whom she united her lot was a member of one of the most illustrious families in Brittany. The union of the young couple was perfect : mutually possessed of lively ardent faith, generosity of soul, attractive piety, they were in perfect unison. They were seen together at the offices of the Church, at the holy table, among the poor, or teaching the catechism to the children and the ignorant. Their house was a heaven upon earth. One should read the correspondence of the two sisters to see the happiness of a truly Christian home, where the harmony is so perfect that the young Irish girl says that her happiness frightens her. " René speaks like an angel of the love of heaven, and that alarms me also. Oh ! how I understand these words of Eugénie de Guérin : ' The heart would immortalize all that it loves ' —that is, the heart likes not separation."*

But soon a thunderclap resounded through the country, and the storm broke upon France ; the legions of the North came down upon her ; the soil was invaded. The young Breton, tearing himself from the tenderness of his wife, departed with his four brothers for the field of battle.

* " Letters of a Young Irishwoman to her Sister."

Hear the words of the young Irish lady:

"René and his brothers are going! O my God! guard them from danger. I love France too well to hinder René from defending her. The fear of grieving me held him back. 'God help us, and have at the English,' as our Breton ancestors used to say. The English of to-day are Prussians. They leave us, five strong valiant brothers, with the courage of lions. . . . Do you remember, Kate, the stories mother used to tell us of the heroism of our grandfather? Do you remember that Georgina, for whom I was named, who said to her brother: 'Go to the battle-field; do not think of me. God and His angels will guard me. Think of your country.' Shall I be less courageous than she? Oh! pray for me. What shall I do without him?"

Not many months after she learns that he is gone from her. Hear again the first cry of this Irish, but at the same time French, heart:

"O René! how proud I am of you—dying on the field of honor after receiving your God in the morning—dying in defence of France! Ah! I would fain have been a Sister of Charity to have the right to receive the last sigh of our courageous defenders.

"Frequently had you said to me: It seems to me that I should have strength to love God even to martyrdom. And a time came when you might have remained by your happy hearth; but your country was in sorrow and you went forth a soldier of right, a soldier of God. Ah! then I felt indeed something break within me.

"Are you mindful in heaven of her who loved you better than herself? Do you remember those delightful days when heavenly love shed a ray from on high upon our love? Do you remember our conversations in which the thought of eternity was ever present? Ah! we both knew truly that our happiness was not of this earth."

And the young widow, forgetting herself and her sorrow at sight of our ever-increasing misfortunes, cries: "O Lord! the happiness of loving Thee, of possessing Thee in heaven, is well worth a few years of Calvary; and although mine at times seems so difficult to ascend, Thou knowest that I weep no longer for myself, but for the *sufferings of René's country, which alone fill my heart.* My poor France, so glorious while she still served Thee, wilt Thou efface her forever from the book of nations, or wilt Thou restore her power? Turn us to Thee, O Christ! who died to save the world, and for the sake of so many hearts that turn to Thee shorten our woes. . . . O my God! have pity on poor France. I offer myself as a holocaust to Thee ; I accept every sacrifice ; I abandon myself into Thy hands. Take with me all devoted souls ; let not France undergo the fate of Ireland ; let her not be crushed by irreligion ; leave her faith and love." Then when she learns the conditions of peace, she sends forth this patriotic cry : " O the Alsatians ! To think that henceforth they belong to the Vandals who have ruined their territory, made a desert everywhere, brought mourning into every home—what infinite grief ! No, the Prussians will not be their master. Alsace is too French at heart. The enemy's yoke may weigh down the body, but it cannot bind the soul. We have here a young wife and mother who has been in the chapel since this morning weeping in despair. Poor Alsace ! What a terrible alternative ! The mother-country sacrificing the most unfortunate sons to purchase the others ! . . . Where is Joan of Arc ? Where are even the women of Carthage ? Lord save us !"

Not many years later she was taken in a few hours from the tenderness of her adopted family, that young Irish girl whose husband's mother spoke of her as " an apparition from heaven, the most loving, devoted, and piously amiable of daughters, an adviser, a refuge, a light to us all."

A few moments before breathing her last she said : " Mother, *I asked that I might die for France;* it was a sacrifice because of leaving you. Now all regret has vanished from my heart ; I am going to see Gertrude, Kate, René, God !" *

Could one believe this was the voice of a stranger ? At sight of such patriotism, such heroism, must we not cry : " Yes, the *Irish faith is French.*"

If there is a place on earth where the faith manifests itself, blossoms instinctively, it is truly upon the tombs of the Apostles, the bones of the martyrs. This is the feeling which fills the soul of the stranger when he visits the catacombs where our saints have prayed, when he respectfully kisses the arena where they fought and shed their blood for Christ. But the feeling is even stronger at the feet of the Sovereign Pontiff, the representative of Jesus Christ among us. It is there that our baptism, so to speak, seems to awake again and speak within us, as nature speaks and reawakens in the presence of our earthly father.† In that land, ever illustrious, men, even the most indifferent, yield in spite of themselves to the religious atmosphere which there surrounds them ; they re-

---

* " Letters of a Young Irishwoman to her Sister."
† Mgr. Pie.

member that they have been baptized. Witness the words of a celebrated writer, the disinterestedness of whose testimony can hardly be doubted : " I kissed with all my heart the wooden cross which is raised in the Coliseum vanquished by the cross. How earnestly the young faith must have clasped it when it there appeared amid the lions and leopards. To-day still, whatever its future may be, the cross, daily more solitary, is it not everywhere the only asylum for the religious soul ?" *

Well it was in Rome itself, the centre of Catholicism, at the feet of Leo XIII., that I was able in my turn to attest the parentage, the admirable similitude, of the *faith of the Irish and the French.*

In the month of May, 1879, there was a rich Irishman from San Francisco, with all his family, at a hotel in Rome. To witness an edifying spectacle you had but to traverse the Corso to the Church of St. Charles, where the father and mother, with their six daughters, were to be found each morning prostrate in prayer, and assisting at mass with Irish fervor.

The head of this family had manifested toward Leo XIII. remarkable generosity, in which only a king of finance could indulge. There-

---

* Michelet's " History of France."

fore, on the eve of their departure from Rome, the Holy Father gave them a special private audience. He devoted a whole hour to them alone.

The Vicar of Him who said, "Suffer little children to come unto me," bestowed particular notice on the youngest child, a little girl of three. He called her to him and said:

"See here, my little one, what souvenir do you wish to receive from the Pope?"

"I would like very much to have your cap."

"But if I give you my cap I will have none for myself."

The objection had been foreseen, and the child at once replied: "Oh! but I shall give you another," and handed him a white cap.

How was such an argument from the lips of such an advocate to be resisted?

The Pope acknowledged himself vanquished, and yielded with a pleasant grace.

"Well, now that you have made me a present I in my turn would like to give you one. Come with me."

And taking the little one by the hand, the Sovereign Pontiff led her into an adjoining apartment and placed a paper in her hand, saying, "Give this to your papa for me."

It was a brief, conferring on the head of the Irish family the title of Chevalier of the Order of St. Sylvester. This charming scene was reproduced on canvas by one of the best painters of Rome. The picture will cross the ocean to perpetuate in the Irish family the memory of one of its happiest days.

About the same period I also witnessed, upon two occasions, at the feet of Leo XIII., the expression of French faith.

On the 2d of May, 1879, I had the happiness of assisting at an audience given to French pilgrims. The Pope was surrounded by ten cardinals and twelve French missionary bishops, who were continuing the great work of the redemption, propagating the faith in the name of France. The Sovereign Pontiff seated himself on the throne in the presence of from five to six hundred of our compatriots, all his devoted children. His Holiness, after hearing the customary address, replied in French. He paid a high tribute to the unceasing labors of the eldest daughter of the Church, praised her past, admired the courage of Catholics of the present day, in spite of obstacles prophesied the glories of her future, congratulated the episcopacy so admirable and so devoted, finally, blessed the families and the whole nation. Each one came in turn to express his faith by prostrating himself at the feet of the successor of Peter. It was truly a beautiful scene, and the tears which welled to the eyes of those present sufficiently attested the general emotion. This, I said to myself, is the most beautiful memory I will bear away with me from Rome. I was mistaken. I had seen the Vicar of Christ, the King of Catholic hearts, *Pontifex Maximus*, upon his temporal throne; I had not seen *il Papa* (the Pope) in all the force of the term, *the Father*. Nor had I seen in all its intensity the complete manifestation of the French faith in presence of this Father *par excellence*.

It was a few days later, the 7th of May, that I witnessed this incomparable spectacle.

It was on this day in fact, at a quarter to seven in the morning, that twenty young persons, from eighteen to twenty-five, silently ascended the stairs of the Vatican. I was one of the four priests who accompanied them, preceded by the Count de Bourcetty, who had recommended them to the Sovereign Pontiff, and before whom the doors of the Vatican opened with pleasing facility. Who, then, were these young people? Young Paris workmen who, at the price of long practiced economy, had come to solicit a blessing from the Pope on their future, their labors, their families, and their patrons. At seven o'clock they were all assembled in the little chapel adjoining the throne-room, where Pius IX. was fond of celebrating the holy sacrifice during the last years of His life. A few moments after, the Pope began the mass, at which these twenty young people had the happiness of receiving Communion from his hand. Another mass followed that of His Holiness. When this was finished the Pope withdrew. Mgr. Macchi, the master of ceremonies, approached us and said, " When you wish you may pass into the throne-room; the Pope will soon return." We followed the prelate, who immediately began to question the young people and to show them the pictures, statues, and objects of art in the room, with an amiability which augured well for the reception which was to follow.

During this time the young people threw some gold pieces on the plate destined to receive the offerings to the Sovereign Pontiff. This offering, the fruit of economy, virtue, and labor, must have been pleasing in the eyes of Him who has said that a glass of cold water will not go unrewarded!

Soon the Pope appeared. They made us a sign to advance, and we were taken to the antechamber itself, adjoining the room where the Pope transacts business, which is usually reserved for cardinals and bishops.

We at once made a circle round the Sovereign

Pontiff, and then began between father and children a beautiful scene which lasted more than an hour. The Pope paused before each of the young men, inquired his name, his condition, his age, his place of residence, even the sum of his daily earnings, with a kindness which surpassed all expression. You should have heard the simple petitions, so full of faith, from these children to their father. One asked a special blessing for his parents. Another, who was an orphan, solicited it for his patron. This one asked a special prayer that Providence would visibly manifest to him the path to follow; that one, finally, that God would favor his plans for the future. And the Father manifested a visible interest in all and everything. He replied to all with caresses and the kindest words, listening as calmly and without any more hurry than if he absolutely had no other occupation.

Nevertheless, the audience was but half over when nine o' clock struck. It was the hour when the Cardinal Minister of State comes to the Sovereign Pontiff in order to give him the intelligence from the different parts of the world which has come during the last twenty-four hours, and to receive his orders for the coming day. It is the most important hour in the Pope's day, the one which he devotes to the important affairs in the government of the Church.

And in fact the hour of nine had hardly sounded when his Eminence Cardinal Nina appeared. Doubtless the Sovereign Pontiff will now end the audience already so long for him, but so short for us. But no; he continues to hear the humble workman, and to do so postpones the discussion of grave Church matters. Ah! in listening to his humble children is he not doing the work of the Church? For since Christ came down from heaven to the straw of the manger, since He espoused poverty as Bossuet has said, since He wielded with His own divine hands the tools of labor, there is no longer any shame in gaining one's bread by the sweat of his brow; Jesus, more than any other, has reëstablished the workman by breaking the chains of pagan slavery.

When the Pope perceived his Eminence Cardinal Nina, he said aloud, "Come, cardinal, come in." The cardinal kissed the Pope's hand in salutation, and said to him in Italian: "Oh! Holy Father, what a beautiful crown you have about you this morning." The Pope replied in French: "Yes, cardinal, truly a beautiful crown; these good French faces please me, for these young people are young French workmen from Paris—sculptors, cabinet-makers, joiners, etc.—who spent their savings to come to see the Pope. They all communicated this morning at my mass, and I wish that they should bear away with them a pleasant memory of their journey. They will say that they received holy Communion from the hand of the Pope, that they were received at the Vatican, and I hope that all their lives they will remember this beautiful day."

The Sovereign Pontiff had finished speaking to each one in particular, when, as if unable to tear himself away from the interesting family, he made them a general address, in which he recommended obedience to parents, submission to patrons, a regular life, love of labor, flight from the occasions of sin and bad companions, when suddenly one of the young men, throwing himself at his feet, said : " Holy Father, I have a favor to ask of you." " Well, what is it, my child?" The young man was so full of emotion that he could scarcely articulate these words : " I ask of your Holiness a special prayer for my father and mother—for the conversion of my parents." At this unexpected act of faith the Pope, taking the young man's head in his arms, silently raised his eyes to heaven. The emotion in the little assembly at this moment reached a climax. Sobs were heard on every side ; one of the workmen in the embrasure of a window could with difficulty restrain his feelings, and almost cried aloud. Cardinal Nina wept, tears came to the eyes of the Pope himself. Why were they not present, those kings of art and great artists; why were not Raphael and Michael Angelo there with their sublime gifts, to put upon canvas this touching scene, so beautiful and yet so sad, that it might remain an imperishable souvenir to posterity? What an admirable picture was that of this young man who, braving all human respect, falls at the feet of the Vicar of Christ, and with sobs asks for his parents the greatest of all gifts, *faith!*

The Sovereign Pontiff, still much moved, held the young man's head in his arms, and said to him: "Have courage, my child! Preach by example in your family; be a model of obedience and Christian virtues. On my part, I promise you the special prayer you solicit for the conversion of your parents. . . . Rise and come with me." And the Pope, still pressing him to his heart, led him into his cabinet, continuing to speak in his ear in a low voice. They returned in a moment, the young man carrying something wrapped in a white handkerchief. "It is a little souvenir," said the Pope," which I bestow upon each of you. Come forward, my children." Each one then advanced in turn and received from the hands of the Sovereign Pontiff a medal bearing the effigy of the Pope in a handsome white box. The distribution was crowned by a general benediction, and we all said to ourselves : This is the end this time ; the kindness of the Holy Father can hardly go further, particularly when we saw him go toward his cabinet.

But no ; this was not all. There was still another scene more paternal than the rest, if possible, which completed the joy of the children and the goodness of the Father ; for hardly had the Sovereign Pontiff left before he reappeared and said : " And now, my young friends, if you would like to see the room and the apartments of the Pope, come in." Imagine our surprise and delight. We immediately entered the Pope's business cabinet ; then the little room adjoining, which serves as a diningroom ; from there to the bedroom, and then to his private library. As we were entering the bedroom, Cardinal Macchi exclaimed : " But, Holy Father, we cannot enter ; the room is not made up." " Well, draw the curtains then," replied the Pope. And there was the Holy Father leading us everywhere, taking us about the apartments, showing us everything with smiling grace, and appearing most pleased at our enjoyment.

On our return he stood at the door of his cabinet, and for the last time gave his ring to be kissed to each one as he passed. We finally withdrew; it was ten o'clock. We had been at the Vatican three hours. Certainly had they followed the promptings of their hearts as they left, they would have cheered enthusiastically to express their joy and gratitude. But what could not be expressed aloud was echoed in their hearts. No, Holy Father, never will these children forget that the Sovereign Pontiff paid to young workmen honors which he does not always bestow upon earthly princes. They will preserve an undying remembrance of this precious day, and prove it by conduct which will be always that of an upright Christian.

As the Sovereign Pontiff took leave of us he said: "If you were not fasting I would offer you a promenade through the Vatican gardens; but you may return during the day. Orders will be given that all the doors shall be opened to you." And in fact, at three o'clock, the young people were admitted to the Vatican gardens, where they spent an hour and a half.

In this beautiful scene of French faith do we not find the principal characteristics of the Irish faith? All human respect was set aside on that day; their faith was demonstrative, active, and generous. Ah! if no efforts were made to destroy these beautiful and precious germs in young hearts they would grow, and the French faith, like her Irish sister, would bring forth admirable fruits.

If the faith of the Irish is French for all these reasons, it is further so because of other characteristics as well ; they have something of the character and spirit of the French. They possess their expansive ardor, patient tenacity, rich imagination, and firm courage ; their vivacity and constancy ; they have particularly that delicate lively repartee always seasoned with that Gallic salt with which they accompany an argument, particularly when it is a question nearly or remotely connected with their religion. The wit then flows naturally, it bubbles up as if from a fountain, and their skill in repartee has become proverbial. Ah ! true faith develops the intellect. We may truly say of her what St. Augustine says of virtue in general : " It develops genius ; it elevates the mind to heavenly things and makes it capable of comprehending all truth."

A stranger one day passed an Irishman working in the country, and thus accosted him : " Pat, can you tell me the distance from here to Boston ?"

Pat, recognizing one who desired to ridicule his nationality, answered :

"But who told you now that my name was Pat?"

"Oh, I guessed it.'

"Then guess the distance from here to Boston."

Two Irishmen walking in the streets of Louisville stopped before a fine new building and examined it on all sides, making their own reflections. In a moment a window opened and the owner angrily ordered them away.

"Upon my word, I thought it was a church," said one.

"So did I," said the other, "until I saw the devil in the window."

An Irishman was one day present at a Protestant religious meeting held outside the city. When the minister of the Gospel took upon himself to say:

"Every one knows that Catholic priests invented confession."

"Every one knows very well that that is a calumny invented by Protestant ministers," cried the Irishman, at the top of his lungs.

There was at once great disturbance in the audience, and many threats against the bold Irishman, with suggestions to show him the door. Order was hardly re-established before the minister resumed:

"Every one knows also that among Catholics indulgences are sold for money."

"Every one knows also that that is another big lie," cried the Irishman again.

At this new correction there was a perfect storm of indignation. Calls to order came from all parts of the house. The minister himself interfered. It was decided to drive from the sacred place the profane intruder who raised his blasphemous voice to contradict the minister of the Gospel. Patrick, possessed of exceptional muscle, made an energetic resistance. He was taken by main force, and four robust men were hardly equal to the task. Outside he refused to walk; so they carried him into the city to deliver him to a policeman as a disturber of divine service. Patrick was being thus borne along in this human vehicle when at the entrance to the city they met a group of Irishmen. Imagine their astonishment, which soon gave place, however, to a perfect volley of jests and loud shouts of laughter.

"What happened to you? Where are you going in such company?"

"Friends," gravely replied Patrick, "I am more honored than was our Lord. At His entry into Jerusalem he was borne upon one ass, and I am carried by four."

A crowd had collected about the singular cortége, and Patrick's words were greeted with loud applause and frantic hurrahs. His bearers, confused and furious, threw their burden on the ground and fled as fast as their legs would carry them. Patrick, abandoned by his first bearers, was at once reconducted in triumph to his house by his compatriots.

Let us quote another page from the *Catholic Herald* of Philadelphia, entitled " Singular Trait of Irish Wit." I give it unabridged, to preserve the originality of the English narrative.

" A controversy took place recently in a street car. An Irishman entered and seated himself opposite a white-cravated individual. The latter seemed to be in a lively humor, for hardly had the new arrival taken his seat than he thus accosted him in a voice loud enough to be heard by all the passengers :

" ' Do you know the news ? '

" ' No, sir,' replied the Irishman ; ' what is it ? Has anything extraordinary happened ? '

"' Something terrible. The bottom fell out of Purgatory, and all the Catholics have fallen into hell.'

" ' Is it possible ? I am very sorry,' replied the Catholic. ' I pity the Protestants below ; they must have been reduced to ashes.'

" The discussion was opened ; the passengers were all attention.

"'You are a minister of the Gospel, are you not?' said the Catholic.

"'Yes, sir, and I am at your service. What can I do to oblige you?'

"'I would like very much to know,' said the Catholic, 'why you have no altars in your churches?'

"'I presume you are an Irishman; therefore, I will answer your question by another. Why have you such costly paintings in your churches, and why are your priests clothed in gorgeous cloth of gold and silver robes?'

"'Do you not know,' said the Catholic, 'that the more ancient a house the more numerous are her treasures and the richer her furnishing? But, my dear sir, would you be good enough to tell me where your Church was before the Reformation?'

"'I again reply after your manner,' said the minister; 'where was your face before it was washed?'

"'I had a purpose in making that remark,' said the Irishman. 'When the Catholic Church, after her labor in converting European nations, recognized that she had contracted some maladies, she applied the remedies Christ had left her; she was healed of all her woes and purified from all stain. Your friend Dean Swift himself explains this truth a little more clearly : " When the Pope cleans his garden, he throws all the weeds over the hedge." No doubt your Reverence understands what he meant by that ?'

" The passengers redoubled their attention. The conductor himself left his platform to follow the discussion, and it was noticed that two or three old ladies who had reached their destinations continued in the car to hear the result of the argument.

" Until now it was the Catholic who had asked the first questions ; the minister thought it was his turn, and proposed one which he considered unanswerable.

" ' Why do you not eat meat on Friday ? Is it not as good on that day as any other ? You must be very foolish to believe otherwise.'

" ' I have not the shadow of an objection to meat ; I like it Friday as much as I do Thursday, and I must confess that if, like you, I had fashioned a religion for myself, I would have freedom to eat meat every day in the week.'

" The audience were much amused at the promptness of the reply ; but the minister posed another question on the same subject which he thought would embarrass his adversary.

" ' Your reply may satisfy you—you and all who think as you do—but your actions contradict your principles. You drink milk on Friday ; the milk comes from a cow. Why can you not as well eat the flesh as drink the milk, since they both come from the same animal ? '

" ' Were you ever a baby ? ' said the Catholic.

" ' There is no reply to such a question.'

" ' Then you drank your mother's milk as much as you wished ? '

" ' Doubtless ; well ? '

" ' Well,' said the Catholic, with a merry smile, ' is that a reason for saying that you have *eaten your mother ?* '

" The laughter which followed this remark could have been heard in all the adjoining streets. All in the car did not share the Catholic's principles ; but his humor was so gay, his arguments so decisive, that every one espoused his side.

" ' You superstitious papists,' replied the minister, tolerably annoyed, ' have no opinion of your own. Your Church leads you by the nose and you believe in what you have never seen.'

" ' Granted,' said the Catholic. ' I could reply that you do the same. There is a difference, however. I allow myself to be guided by the Church which Jesus Christ has founded. I believe what she teaches, while you permit yourself to be guided by apostate priests or monks whom the Church has rejected from her bosom for their pride and disobedience. As to believing in things which I have not seen, I am unlike you in this respect, for you believe that you are possessed of brains and common sense, and yet neither you nor any one else has ever seen them.'

"' But you,' replied the minister, 'believe absurdities ; you believe in the sacrifice of the mass ; you believe that the priest can remit sin ; you believe that the saints can hear you ; you believe in the existence of the devil. All this is absurd ; such things are culpable follies in the eyes of men of good sense. Show me the devil and I will give you fifty dollars.'

"' Don't get so excited, my dear friend,' said the Catholic. 'What you call absurd I believe because it is the Word of God and the teaching of the Church. I believe it because they are truths revealed by God. As to your last objection, my belief in the devil, keep your money for yourself ; have patience to wait a time. Change neither your life nor your faith and I give you my word you will see the devil for nothing.'

"The argument was decisive ; the minister got more than he asked. He was desirous of making a new effort to regain the sympathy of the auditors.

"' Your Church is so opposed to liberty,

which is so natural to us ; and her doctrines are not Christian. She admits the truth of no other sect, and sends every man to hell who is not of her communion. I wish you to clearly declare it before our hearers : Do you believe that there is no salvation outside the Catholic Church ? '

" ' Certainly I believe it. There is but one God ; consequently there must be but one religion. This religion was figured by the Ark, and as those who were saved from the deluge had to enter this ark, so those who wish to be saved at their death must during their lives belong to the Church which Jesus Christ our Lord has founded.'

" ' Then all those who do not belong to it will go to hell ? '

" ' If that is your opinion, so be it ; you particularly, who have no other place to assign them.'

" ' Now, sir, let us go further, for I wish to prove to these people here how little charity you and your Church have. I require you to answer my question categorically : Do you think that I will go to hell after my death ? '

" ' Oh ! my dear sir,' replied the Catholic ; ' nothing is further from my thoughts ; I never imagined such a thing.'

" ' But,' said the minister, ' what is there special in me, or what quality do I possess capable of exempting me from the fate reserved for all the others?'

"'*Invincible ignorance!*' exclaimed the Irishman, rising and leaving the car with an indescribable smile of satisfaction.

"The passengers applauded vigorously mid shouts of laughter, while the minister escaped in confusion by the front platform.

"As he was leaving a gentleman remarked aloud that *invincible ignorance* was a very poor means of being saved, and added that he was willing to bet that for the future the white-cravated gentleman would never be heard to say again that the 'bottom had fallen out of purgatory.'"

Since these two peoples, the French and the Irish, have so much resemblance and sympathy, since they are a people of brothers in so many respects, why has not France, like Ireland, preserved intact the precious treasure of faith? It so well becomes the French whose country was born Catholic of a victory due to the God of Clotilde; baptized Catholic at Reims with the holy water poured on the head of Clovis by St. Remi; the country which, after all, and in spite of everything, will continue with her sword or her influence to accomplish the *Gesta Dei per Francos.**

* Acts of God through the French.

"Oh, my country," will I cry with one of the most illustrious victims of the commune tigers, "you who were born at Tolbrai of a victory and an act of faith; you whom religion and war, uniting with the cross and the sword, bore upon a royal shield and presented to young Europe as their chief, their model, and almost their monarch; you who went through the world and traversed fifteen centuries with the beautiful and grand qualities of a soldier, with the zeal of a missionary, with the heroism of a Sister of Charity; O my country, preserve your Christian traditions, and remain faithful to your glorious past!" *

As I am completing this modest work Ireland is again going through a sorrowful crisis; she is struggling with the horrors of famine. The misery of the farmers makes it absolutely impossible for them to make any provision for the failure of the crops. The humble garden or little corner of land has produced nothing; the great farms are sterile; there is no bread in the cabin, no potatoes in the pit, no work, and consequently no possibility of procuring strict necessities.

All this would be very little if that terrible law of *eviction* was not, like the sword of Dam-

* Mgr. Darboy, "Allocution à la Fin de la Station de l'Avent," 1867.

ocles, ever suspended over the head of the poor tenant, who has no legal redress against the landlord. The latter, whenever he chooses, can evict his tenant by withdrawing his word, the only security he gives him, and with which the Irishman must be content. It is very certain that in the middle of the nineteenth century, to the shame and astonishment of our European economists, a people very near us are dying of hunger.

As in preceding misfortunes, Ireland remembers that she is the sister of France; it is to her she cries. Here is the appeal for succor which a few weeks since was made with tears by an Irish religious, a Joan of Arc in her way. She is moved at the woes of her country, and she endeavors to wrest her compatriots from the horrible tortures of famine. She thus addresses herself to the French Catholics :

"Convent, Kenmare, County Kerry, Ireland.

"*To the Editor of the Univers:*

" France and Ireland are both tried. In Ireland we have, as you know, famine; in your dear France you are suffering a spiritual affliction—a famine, might we say, of the fear of God. Can we not at least aid and comfort one another together? Yes, certainly; already you have begun the " good work," and generous France has dried the tears of many poor people and little ones here tortured by hunger. What can the Irish religious say to you but that in her heart France occupies the first place after Ireland, and that she prays much at sight of the persecution which threatens religion and religious orders in France? If I speak as a suppliant it will be because my soul is wrung by the appeals which come to me from priests and religious in behalf of their poor, sick, and dying. However considerable the amount already collected by the relief committee, it should be ten times the sum to meet our present misery. Moreover, the public committees give to the starving only *Indian meal*, a coarse food which in England is given only to dogs and horses; and even these animals have other food with it, while our starving poor are allowed nothing more.

"Now I am sure that if the poor of Ireland are condemned to this diet of *Indian meal*—and it is the only food of tens of thousands—the pest will follow. Remember that they have no milk for the sick and dying, nor butter, nor eggs, nor vegetables. The effect of this diet is already visible in a great deal of sickness. I appeal then to your Christian charity in behalf of my subscription. . . . Alas! if abundant succor does not come to us again, and come quickly, Ireland will be a prey to epidemics from one end of the land to the other. But I know I do not address myself in vain to French hearts. Mothers in the midst of your children, think how you would feel if your little ones asked with tears for a little bread and you had it not to give them. Bishops of France, my fathers, you who have already done so much for Ireland, will you not see if in the goodness of your hearts you cannot do still a little more? My fathers, priests, so devoted to France, you will not refuse to hear a poor religious who pleads but for the priests of Ireland, so like you in their faith, their patience, their love for their country. My sisters, religious of France, I hold out my arms to you as my sisters of Ireland extend their arms to me. The little which the children of your schools will give will do so much good. We will do our best to make a return for it with our prayers, our tears, our intercession in behalf of that France which is hardly less dear to us than to you.

"Your sister and servant in the love of the Immaculate Heart of Mary,

"SISTER MARY FRANCIS CLARE."

May what I have said of Ireland, and particularly of the similarity of the Irish and the French faith, suggest to some charitable souls the thought of lending a favorable ear to the Nun of Kenmare's appeal, so Christian, so French, so patriotic! May a few alms from our superfluity reach her monastery, and go from her hands and heart to those who suffer and who die of hunger.

No ; France does not and cannot forget what poor Ireland—as grieved and afflicted as if our woes were her own—did for us at the news of our recent disasters. Did she not send us her sons who shed their blood for us ; did she not send us the assistance of her ambulances and, through the mite of the poor much more than offerings of the rich, the magnificent *alms of more than a million !*

CHAPTER XVI.

SOULS THE TRUE RICHES OF A PEOPLE—TRUE PROGRESS THROUGH THE TEACHINGS OF CHRIST—HEROISM OF THE CHRISTIAN BROTHERS DURING THE FRANCO-PRUSSIAN WAR.

WE have dwelt at some length upon the *wonders of the Irish faith.*

Protestants who have apostatized from the faith of their ancestors endeavor to justify their criminal separation. They loudly proclaim their material prosperity; they display to the eyes of all the splendor of their fortune, their welfare, and their comfort, and they reproach Ireland with her poverty as a malediction from heaven.

They are easily answered. The poverty of the nation, so far from being ignominious, is rather a new ray added to her glorious aureole. Did not Jesus Christ come from "the abode of the angels to espouse poverty and to have a great number of sons who should be perfect?" * Was it not He who beatified poverty: "Blessed are the poor?"

* St. Francis of Assissi.

After the example of her divine Founder, the Church, faithful guardian of the Gospel, continues to look upon this earth as the path of the traveller ; she reminds the Christian that it is a place of passage where he may erect the tent of a day, but not think to abide forever. Behold why her most illustrious children are the most detached souls, the voluntary poor ! With their eyes fixed on the manger and Calvary, they say with St. Francis of Sales : ' Soon we will be in eternity ; we shall see then how little important were the affairs of this world, how little it mattered whether they were accomplished or not accomplished."

The principle laid down by Jesus Christ is as necessary to the life of a nation as to that of each individual soul.

Let it not be believed, however, that this profound contempt for perishable things, these elevations of the soul toward heaven, render it a stranger or indifferent to legitimate material progress. God forbid that it should be necessary to deny the conquests over nature, to despise the value of the progress in sciences and arts ; that one must refuse to admire modern inventions, those glorious results of human genius !

But this is not everything. We must truly recognize that there exist elements superior, though much less visible. That these supernatural elements being wanting, in vain we construct magnificent palaces, enlarge the precincts of our great cities, cover the world with a network of railway and telegraph ; all this, admirable progress by itself—that is, if it have no other end than the development of material prosperity--is condemned in advance. It infallibly leads to decadence and ruin. A society thus constituted lacks the superior principle essential to life ; mind is stifled under this weight of matter.

Nevertheless this is not what occupies the minds of to-day. "Is it not evident that the world has lost its nobility? That the noble aims of former days, now called chimerical and barbarous, are succeeded by the humblest and most realistic cares! Ye great minds of Europe, busy yourselves deciding which nation manufactures best silk or cotton." *

The same author has written these significant lines on Rome · "Why is Rome one of those places of the world where one is best elevated to the sentiments of great and beautiful things? Because material life is almost effaced there. The day when the petty customs of European civilization there become dominant, the day

---

* Renan, " La Poésie de l'Exposition."

when shops copied from boulevards replace the poor bazaars of the *Place Navone*, or factory chimneys smoke on the Aventine, Rome—I mean the Rome dear to all who think and feel, the city of the soul, as Byron calls it—will cease to exist."

This same thought was developed in the *Revue des Deux Mondes* of June, 1855:

"We have an essentially prosaic and vulgar mode of judging at the present day. We weigh, we measure people, race, objects, as we weigh oil, or as we measure stuffs. A man has only a productive and commercial value. . . . The first nation of the world is that one which manufactures best or sells most. . . . The Celtic race seem to persist in living in order to show that there is something preferable to the bondage of that hunger and thirst for riches, for power, for labor itself, and that a mystic monk, barefooted, travel-stained but penetrated with the principles of the Gospel, may in the scale of souls be superior to the honors of wealth, to power, even to the Czar Nicholas, the representative of power, even to Benjamin Franklin, the useful and virtuous citizen."

The same author remarks, a few pages further on : " Great economists, learned authors of treatises on railroads, . . . opulent representatives of all that is material and vulgar, uncover the head for once as you pass these hungry ragged mendicants; for these mendicants represent an ideal which has never been realized on earth: that of Christian and mystic chivalry, the protection of the weak by the strong, the ideal of disinterestedness, of devotion, of holy activity." The Irish, he adds, are exempt from this thraldom which characterizes triumphant nations.*

At sight of the petty frivolities of luxury, the smoke and bustle of the various industries, new streets, enlarged boulevards, grander and more commodious dwellings, one experiences the desire to repeat with Bossuet, " The true riches of a people are souls!"

Then, "when men are inspired with superior gifts of faith, when hearts are vowed to abnegation, when they know not how to stoop to dishonor, when the austere and glorious path of sacrifice is known to all, when individual energies are united in a virile and fruitful solidity, when generous and Christian ideas form the blood which flows in a nation, is it not a great people?"†

When the rapid acquisition of wealth at any price has become a doctrine, when the passion

---

* C. Montegu, *Revue des Deux Mondes*, June, 1855.

† Mgr. Mermillod, "Discours en faveur des pauvres d'Irelande."

for possessions is formulated into a system and declared an essential element of social life, when all are more or less slaves to that absorbing and degrading pursuit of national welfare, is it not beautiful to see a people whom misery cannot degrade, whom poverty ennobles, and who in spite of and against everything, with the strength of God Himself, persist by the energy of their faith in preaching the superiority of heaven over earth, of soul over matter, of eternity over time! At the same time, let us beware of supposing such a people an enemy to *progress!*

They love, they admire, they seek this progress, for to them it is a law, a duty; it is the law of a Christian. His faith obliges him to pursue, to make progress in good, not only every day of his life, but every moment from the cradle to the tomb.

What can our utilitarians, with only their principles of material progress, do for the solution of the great problems of the day? What can they do to obviate the suffering and alleviate the miseries of humanity? At one time they tell us: "A little more progress in industries, and the world shall be safe from famine." And let the sun but avert its rays for a time, let the flood gates of heaven be opened a short period, nations at once begin to fear.

Another time they have said: "Still a little more progress in medicine, and men and plants will be safe from the pestilent maladies which afflict the world." And behold each year the mysterious scourge, hidden in the depth of the soil or in our humanity, like the sleeping lion of the forest suddenly awakes and cries to the alarmed population, "Beware, I am come!" Again they have said: "A little more progress in civilization, and nations shall henceforth enjoy eternal peace." And at every moment, if we but listen, we hear in some portion of the globe the clash of arms, the roar of cannon, the crackling of the *mitrailleuse.* Yes, war! And frequently not only the war of people against people, nation against nation, but brother against brother—civil, fratricidal war!

No, alone they can do nothing; their impotence is but too manifest. "Far from you," writes a modern savant in 1859, "far from you that unhappy philosophy which preaches materialism and atheism as new doctrines destined to regenerate the world; they destroy . . . but they regenerate not." *

In material progress relying on faith, behold the fruitful source of life; behold where are found infallible remedies for the evils which afflict humanity.

* Cousin.

Then let this Catholic faith come to you. It will bring you its incomparable institutions so grandly devoted, so resplendent in the consuming fire of their charity. The abandoned, the sick, the orphaned child, the poor, the aged, the captive, the insane, the innocent, the guilty, and even the criminal shall all find consolation, a refuge, an asylum.

Receive among you the *Brothers of St. John of God;* they fly to the succor of the insane.

Receive *St. Vincent of Paul*, escorted by his spiritual daughters, hastening to succor the miseries of the poor. Did they not recently exhibit to our astonished age the heroism of charity struggling on the battle-field side by side with the heroism of the soldier?

Receive among you our *Little Sisters of the Poor*, gathering in the streets the abandoned, the aged, who blaspheme and cry : " There is no Providence, for I am hungry and cold, and my children cast me from them since the day when I ceased to furnish my share of toil or wages."

Send not from your midst *those souls consumed with the love of God*, who by a life of recollection, prayer, and penance avert the divine wrath. Even as the lightning rod turns aside the lightning, they avert from you the wrath enkindled by the innumerable crimes which corrupt the world.

Banish not from the soil of your country the *Members of the Society of Jesus*, those incomparable professors for youth! Their science and their virtues alone are capable of forming generations in whom nobility of sentiment rises to the height of intelligent devotion.

Reject not the admirable *Christian Brothers*, those masters so modest, so devoted, and so dear to children; those men of such generous patriotism.

During our recent trouble they were seen everywhere braving the fire of battle to assist the wounded and the dying. From the height of the capital's defences, General Ducros, moved by their heroism, cried out: " Stop, friends! Go no further! Religion and country ask no more."

Finally, let the *Catholic priesthood* come among you to elevate your souls by divine teachings, and form them to the practice of justice and virtue. They also, they above all, the priests of Jesus Christ Saviour of men, know how to devote themselves, like their Divine Master, to the salvation of their brothers; they know how to stand face to face with death in the midst of public pestilence, and to struggle, even when its desolation is universal, to wrest from it its victims. Yesterday these men were called Charles Borromeo or Belzunce; to-morrow they will bear another name; but whatever names they bear, it is in the ranks of the priesthood that the truest friends of mankind are ever found, that devotion is carried to voluntary sacrifice of life, even to martyrdom if necessary.

One August morning in 1878, when the yellow fever was at its height, a little child in New Orleans was seen sadly wandering in one of those large avenues usually so brilliant and gay, but then as solitary and silent as death itself. The child was scarcely clothed, his eyes were full of tears, and his grief found vent in heart-rending sobs. Alas! he was asking himself where he should find a morsel of bread for the day that was before him, or who would give him shelter for the coming night.

A pious lady passed at this moment. She was deeply moved at the child's appearance, and divining the trouble, approached him and said, with motherly tenderness and sweetness :

"What is the matter, my poor child? Why are you weeping so bitterly?"

"Ah! then you are not afraid of me, madam?" said the child.

"And why should I be afraid of you?"

"Because my father and mother and my little brothers and sisters have all just died of yellow fever; now everybody flies from me, they do not want to see me anywhere, and I do not know where to go. . . . Ah, madam, I am very unhappy," he said, while his sobs redoubled.

"Well, my little friend, be consoled," said the lady, taking him by the hand. "I promise you I will not fly from you; I will not be afraid of you. I have also known sorrow, death has visited my home; but come with me, my house shall be your home; come, I will be your mother until it pleases God to send us better days."

Noble-hearted woman! Ah! the angels must have smiled at sight of the heroism of her charity, and God from heaven above must have shed upon her all the blessings He reserves for the protector of the abandoned orphan.

Is there need to say who this woman was? It was she whom the whole city knew as the model of all Christian virtues; it was the woman of the Gospel; it was faith and charity in action.

Side by side with such a scene let the enthusiastic admirers of modern materialism now exhibit their works.

We know what recently happened in Geneva in the midst of an epidemic. Other ministers took flight, having first decided by lot which one should remain at his post. According to their rule, *one alone* was sufficient.

Ah! devotion is the sublime privilege of faith, and of people who possess faith! Surely a nation so rich in works before God and man should not be reproached for her poverty. Yes, eloquent defender of Ireland, you had reason to cry to the *élite* of Parisian society: "The first powers of our age, the two most rich and illustrious, are a dethroned prince and a people in rags: Pius IX. extends his royal hand to you and Ireland asks you for bread."*

---

* Mgr. Mermillod à l'Église Ste. Clotilde.

CHAPTER XVII.

LEVER OF ARCHIMEDES—MACAULAY—LACORDAIRE—IRELAND—POLAND.

"ARCHIMEDES asked but a lever and fulcrum to raise the world ; but in his time the lever and the fulcrum were unknown. They are now known. Faith is the lever, and the point of rest is the breast of the Lord Jesus." *

Never were there truer or more beautiful words! It is faith which elevates the world. In fact, is not faith the lever of a people? Is it not for them the most precious of all blessings? Is it not faith which gives them happiness, strength, and glory? I will go further, and dare to say it is faith which preserves the life of a nation, even though she be mutilated, bleeding, martyred—whether she be called Poland or Ireland.

"Not only during one, or even twenty administrations, but for centuries we have used the sword against Irish Catholics," says a cele-

---

* Lacordaire's Conferences.

brated historian. "We have tried famine, we have had recourse to every artifice of Draconian laws ; we have attempted unlimited extermination, not to abase or conquer an abhorred race but to efface every trace of this people from the land of their birth. But what has been the result? Have we suceeded? We have failed to exterminate or even weaken them. They have successively increased. . . . I know history, I have studied history ; but I confess my inability to find in it a satisfactory explanation of this fact. . . . But were I to find myself in St. Peter's at Rome, and could I with the faith of a Catholic read the inscription on its dome : *Thou art Peter, and upon this rock I will build my Church; the gates of hell shall not prevail against it*, then I could understand the problem of the history of Ireland."

If the celebrated historian during his stay in Rome had not contented himself with reading the inscriptions in the dome of St. Peter's ; if, traversing the grand basilica of the world he had sought to better inform himself, he would have found the completion of his thought and the solution of the great problem in two inscriptions on the confessionals, which cannot be read without deep emotion : *Gens Hiberna! Gens Polona!* (Irish nation! Polish nation!)

What does that mean if not that in the eyes

of faith, in the eyes of the Church, these two sister martyr nations still live. Let diplomacy, let conquerors, let the so-called sages of the age, with disdainful indifference efface if they will the names of these noble nations from the map of the world. The holy Catholic Church—the citadel of justice, the asylum of right, the rampart of the weak oppressed by brute force—the Catholic Church sacredly preserves, as in a reliquary, beside the tomb of the Apostles, in the very centre of Catholicity, those great names as an immortal souvenir, as a sweet and imperishable hope.

CHAPTER XVIII.

THE ANCIENT PROBLEM—ITS SOLUTION, THE DECALOGUE — JOUFFROY — INCREDULITY TENDS TO DEPOPULATE HEAVEN AND DISENCHANT EARTH.

AT the present time the world is everywhere seeking constitutions capable of advancing and giving life to nations, of affording happiness to society, to families, to individuals. Ah! the only constitution which can effect this prodigy, realize such a dream, is as old as the world: it is the Decalogue—that is, Faith. Nations, families, and individuals will only find again the happiness they seek everywhere and find nowhere, when they seek it at its veritable source, when they learn anew to make the sign of the cross, and to conform their lives to the lessons of the catechism, to the maxims of our old creed, which alone gives true science and true happiness. "How live in peace when one knows not whence he came, whither he is going, what he is to do here below; when all is a mystery, an enigma full of doubt and fear! To live in peace in such ignorance is a *contradiction and an impossibility!*" *

The philosopher whom I have just cited unfortunately was a victim of doubt; nevertheless he taught others the means of acquiring this desirable peace and avoiding the *contradiction* which caused him so much suffering. The following well-known page is also from him. It cannot be read without emotion when we remember that he by whom it was so well written points out a sure path which he himself refused to follow.

"There is a little book," he tells us, "which children are made to learn, and upon which they are questioned in the church. Read this little book, which is the Catechism; you will find in it the solution of all the questions I have proposed, all without exception. Ask the Christian whence came the human species. He knows. Ask whither it is tending. He will tell you. Ask that poor child, who never in his life has thought about it, why he is here below; and what will become of him after his death; he will give you a sublime reply, which he will not understand, but which is no less admirable. Ask him how and for what end the world was created; why God placed in it plants and

---

* Jouffroy, "Mélanges Philosophiques."

animals ; how the earth was peopled ; if it was by one or by several families ; why men speak various tongues ; why they suffer, why they struggle, and how all this will end. He knows the origin of the world, the origin of the human species, the question of races, the destiny of man in this life and the next, man's relation with God, the duties of man toward his fellow-beings, the rights of man over creation. Upon none of these questions is he in ignorance ; and when he is grown he will hesitate no less upon natural rights, upon political rights, the rights of the people ; for all this springs, all this, clearly and spontaneously as it were, flows from Christianity. Behold what I call a great religion ! I recognize it by this sign : it leaves no question unsolved which concerns the interests of mankind." *

It is because they have rejected the sublime teachings of "*that little book which is the catechism*" that, under the breath of unchained passions, breeding disorganization everywhere, society is crumbling to its base. But when we reject religious dogmas we must not dream of imposing political doctrine. Without faith in God there is no faith in man ; and when the churches are empty the prisons are full. When

* Jouffroy.

we close the cloister and drive forth its saints, we must enlarge the doors of our jails. We must create at a distance convict colonies to give an asylum to these unhappy beings who leave our prisons, punished no doubt by human law, but unchanged in spirit. They continue to bear in their hearts the criminal fire which consumes them; because they are not men of faith. "Be assured that incredulity depopulates heaven and disenchants earth."*

Oh! men of progress, inventors of new systems, you agitate all possible subjects, you discuss anew questions long since solved, you desire above all to master the problem of happiness. Then adopt the means. Build upon that sacred, that infallible rock; dig not unwholesome springs when you have at hand the source of living waters; cause religion to flourish in souls; give faith anew to the people, and you will have a peaceful and happy society, for where faith triumphs the rich find their happiness in making others happy and comforting the poor, while the laborer ceases to curse his poverty and toil. "If at times his burden weighs heavily upon him, he raises prayerful eyes and hands to heaven, and is strengthened and consoled. When he hungers, and suffers, faith

---

* Scherer, "Mélanges Philosophiques," p. 182.

shows him his God, who suffers with him on the cross. If remorse weighs him down, *faith* gives him a priest to receive the heavy secrets of his heart. And when his limbs refuse him service, *faith* sends him a Sister of Charity to ease his sufferings and honor his soul in the anguish of his body. He is resigned, because he loves God and hopes; and the rich can live and sleep in peace without fear of being awakened by the discontented murmurings of the populace." *

"Father," wrote a celebrated captive from the depth of his prison in Venice, "all my sorrows are lightened since the day I came into possession, here, of the first of all blessings, *religion*, which the turbulence of the age had almost caused me to lose. †

---

* Marchal, "L'homme comme il faut."
† Silvio Pellico. His letters.

CHAPTER XIX.

THE ENEMIES OF FAITH—WHAT FAITH HAS DONE FOR THEM.

CONCLUDE. Should these humble pages fall into the hands of one of those men, at present so numerous, who are enemies of faith without perhaps any conscious motive for their enmity, may I be permitted to say to them, with great liberty doubtless, but with still more of the charity of the apostle:

"Why are you an enemy of faith? What crime has she been guilty of against you? What injury has she done you? For which of her works do you condemn her?"

On the day of your birth the Catholic Church, by the sound of her bells, saluted your entrance into the world; she received you with joy into her temple; she poured the baptismal water on your head, and returned you to your parents with the innocence and beauty of the angels —that is, with two further claims upon their love and devotion. As the years of your childhood went on, was it not faith which gave you the most beautiful days of your life, the sweetest joys of your heart? Do you remember your first Communion and the many other happy days of that time, when you needed, as it was said, but "wings to take your flight to heaven." You are now the head of a family. Tell me, who instructs your children to-day? Who welcomes them with happiness, who guides them, who loves them, and daily teaches them to love you, to respect you, to honor you, to obey you, that they may *live long in the land.* Who does this? Always *faith* under the figure of the priest, the Christian Brother or the Sister of Charity!

Later, though always too soon, when sorrow comes to you, when a cruel sickness prostrates you on a bed of suffering, when perhaps your frightened children fly from you, who will you have at your pillow, who will faithfully stand at your bedside? Who will die for you, if necessary, at the sacred post of duty and devotion? Always *faith* under the figure of a priest or a religious. Finally, when your eyes are closed in death, when your relatives and friends have left you, when your coffin is deserted, who will charitably receive your remains? Always *faith*, or the Catholic Church. She will go with respect even to your home to seek your body ; she will bring it in triumph to her temple ; she will burn incense about it, an honor which she renders to God alone ; with the tenderness of a mother she bends in prayer over it, and bears it to its last dwelling.

Finally, when in the tomb you are sleeping your last sleep, when all this world is ended for you, when you are everywhere forgotten, when perhaps your name is no longer uttered, when they have ceased to visit your tomb, to mourn your death even in that little corner of earth which you loved so well, there will still be one who does not forget you. The Church—that is, *faith*—will be always mindful of you ; she will bid her priests suspend for a moment the holy sacrifice of the mass to piously remember you before God ; until the end of ages, as long as the world exists, *faith* will daily ask God to give you a "*place of refreshment, light and peace.*"

Since *faith* lavishes upon you all the tender care of a good mother, why will you not all have for her the sentiments of devoted children ? The face of the earth would then be changed, our exile here below would be a foretaste of heaven ; the great problem of the world would be solved ; the dream would be realized ; we should be in the possession, as far as it is possible here below, of *happiness*.

Then let the enemies of our faith sound their

hearts. How many among them would be obliged to say, if they were sincere : " Born of pious parents, and in a country where the Catholic faith was still ardent, I had been early accustomed to consider man's future and the care of his soul the most important affair of my life ; and my education moreover had contributed to strengthen me in these serious dispositions. For a long time the beliefs of Christianity fully met all the wants and all the anxieties which such dispositions awaken in the soul. These questions—to me the only ones meriting the consideration of man—the religion of my fathers answered, and these answers I believed ; and, thanks to my belief, the present life was clear to me ; and on the other hand, I beheld unfolding before me the cloudless future which must follow it. At peace about the path I was to follow in this world, tranquil about the end to which it must lead me in the next, understanding the phases of life and death which unite them, understanding myself, knowing the designs of God for me, and loving Him for the goodness of His designs, I was happy with that happiness which comes from an ardent and firm faith in a doctrine which solves all the great questions which can interest humanity." *

* Jouffroy, " Nouveaux Mélanges Philosophiques."

If in tracing these few pages I have been able to awaken a similar remorse in the heart of one of our brothers, to force this cry from his troubled conscience, to cause him to make this acknowledgment, provided it be followed by a practical resolution, that of returning to religion whom we approach as a mother, "whom we leave at the first success and who awaits us at the first tear,"* I shall be amply recompensed for this humble labor, I will have attained my end—the end which above all every priest of Christ should propose to himself: THE GREATER GLORY OF GOD AND THE SALVATION OF SOULS.

* Aug. Cochin.

www.ingramcontent.com/pod-product-compliance
Lightning Source LLC
Chambersburg PA
CBHW021842230426
43669CB00008B/1055